PERIOD LIGHTING FIXTURES

Fig. I. Candeliero Veneziano of the
Eighteenth Century

PERIOD
LIGHTING FIXTURES

By

Mr. & Mrs. G. GLEN GOULD

WITH ILLUSTRATIONS

NEW YORK : DODD, MEAD & COMPANY

MCMXXVIII

PRINTED IN U. S. A.

MANUFACTURED IN THE UNITED STATES OF AMERICA
BY THE VAIL-BALLOU PRESS, INC., BINGHAMTON, N. Y.

To

MR. RICHARDSON WRIGHT

whose kindness and encouragement has made this work possible,

we gratefully dedicate it.

MR. and MRS. G. GLEN GOULD

INTRODUCTION

An introduction, we take it, is something that writers write *after* they have written a book, and being full of their subject "spill over" a bit, or even exuberantly with all or somewhat they have left unsaid. "Out of the fullness of the heart the mouth speaketh"—was an intimate secret known long ago to a very wise man of the Near East. But this fullness is very full indeed, in our case, and it seems like taking an unfair advantage of any reader to unburden ourselves at the *end* of our work, at the point where we expect the reader to *start* to garner what we have widely gleaned.

Besides, the field is a new one or almost so. Allemagne has done wonders for France, but see what he had at hand to work with! What nation has taken greater pains to keep a record of her own accomplishments! Hayward has done fine work in collecting a mass of material in his "Colonial Lighting Fixtures" the reprint of which we recently reviewed, but—

We leave the final word to the reader. If you know Allemagne, and Hayward, and Macquoid in his Dictionary of English Furniture, you will know how to finish the sentence we have left up in the air with a *but*—. If you do not know them all, you will form your own conclusions anyway.

Last: It is a labor of love. Nothing but the joy of the work could repay the long hours of research that have been succinctly compressed often into a paragraph.

In fairness we must express our gratitude to Mr. Richardson Wright, Editor of *House & Garden* in which the meat of these articles originally appeared. We are grateful for his respect for our work. We are grateful that there are such persons as Mr. Milton Samuels and Mr. Emile Gallet in the world, willing under all circumstances to share, with an amiability that is constantly astonishing, their accumulated knowledge of antiques. We are thankful for Mr. William Clifford of The Metropolitan Museum and Mr. Oliver Barton of The New York Public Library for their fluent knowledge of books and their quick readiness to put a knowing finger on a needed page or paragraph.

We are happy if these chapters serve you or enlarge your horizon of perception of the beauty that is good.

MR. AND MRS. G. GLEN GOULD

February 1, 1928.

CONTENTS

PERIOD LIGHTING FIXTURES

CHAPTER I

ITALY

Iᴛ is difficult for us to imagine the world of pre-Renaissance days in Italy, when there was little knowledge of the classic arts of Greece and only fading traditions of those of Rome. It was not until the 16th Century that Michael Angelo stumbled upon that bit of fine old Roman sculpture that led to the digging up of buried treasure, and set artists further aflame with the inspiration already spread abroad by Brunelleschi which we call the Renaissance, and which still continues to illumine the work of designers as well as sculptors and painters.

In pre-Renaissance Italy we must shut our eyes to the beauty of many things familiar to us as Italian, in fact to almost all that we are apt to think characteristically Italian. Venice in her early thriving trade with the Orient brought in unusual wares, especially from the Near East, and spread westward the Saracenic element in decoration. Sicily, so near the mainland, was occupied by the Saracens themselves, and this influence was established there in the 9th Century, linking their productions closely with those of the Moors in their occupancy of Spain a century earlier. It was in the 13th Century that Marco Polo made his memorable visit to China, journeying through the Near East, and returning to tell his tale to Italy and the world, so strange a tale that it was long thought fabulous. But Sir Aurel Stein in our own century followed Polo's line of travel, proving its accuracy and locating rich archæological treasures.

So acceptable were the suave and lovely wares from the Orient, and so little were they understood in the 12th Century that the pierced metal hanging lamp of the Mohammedan mosque hung without scruple in the Italian Christian cathedral. The typical Saracenic candle cup or socket shared the popularity of the spike or pricket at least as early as the 13th Century. Sockets and prickets of a sort had a very ancient origin.

Lighting the house in Italy was never a serious affair until modern ideas of civilization began the stupendous task of turning night into day. The more or less even distribution of daylight and dark throughout the twenty-four hours in the zone of the Mediterranean countries gave no great impetus to artificial illumination. All the ancient world went to bed with the sun and got up with him, and needed other light only for extraordinary work or special occasion. The little hand lamp sufficed for prolonged work, and was multiplied and abetted by other means for the unusual occasion.

Such household lighting fixtures as date in this pre-Renaissance period are quite simple. Oil and candles were both in use. Servants held torches at table or carried them abroad to light the way at night. The torch holder—*torciere,* the large and the small candlestick—*candelabro* and *candeliere,* similar in design: the lanterns —*lanterna* and *lampione,* and the lamp—*lampada,* about complete the list of fixtures. Lamps were more generally used than candles though candles were not uncommon as early as the 6th Century.

The little hand lamp was as useful in ancient Egypt, China, Greece, and Rome as in Colonial America, and received much attention from craftsmen of every country and age, until progress in modes of lighting with gas and electricity made it useless. In pre-Renaissance Italy it was often conceived in the grotesque and animal forms common to the days of Roman splendor. But these lamps cannot be compared either in design or workmanship with the beautiful bronze lamps set up on tripods or hung on the elaborate candelabra which lit up the revelings of decadent Rome, though they do often hark back in their simple forms to those carried by the courageous Christians to their precious meetings in the gruesome catacombs underlying the City.

In the 11th and 12th Centuries, metal-work like other materials still showed the Saracenic touch in Sicily and southern Italy, at a time when northern Italy responded to the combined Romanesque and Byzantine influences. Byzantine art ideas were spread by returning Crusaders and traders, although they had already appeared as early as the 7th Century. The wonderful bronze candlestick known as the *Albero*—the dove, in the Milan Cathedral, is an example of this dual influence. It was made in the late 12th or early 13th Century, but its origin is still in dispute. The workmanship is evidently not Italian. Large fixtures for the decoration of churches were increasingly used after their first introduction when ceremonious ritual replaced the earlier simple worship of the first centuries of the Christian Era. The enormous hanging light of Pope Adrien I dates from the 8th Century. Suspended lamps in the sanctuary became more general in the 9th Century, while the *coronas*—crowns of light, so superb in Gothic France were known also to Italy at this time.

There was no sharp distinction made between fixtures for the church and those for the home. When at all elaborate, ecclesiastical fixtures were ornamented with Christian emblems, the lily, the crown, the cross, etc., but this kind of adornment was not thought out of place for the home, more particularly if that home were pretentious, especially if it were a palace. Even so the grotesques which we might think distinctly secular were freely used for church adornment. The fondness for grotesques is not absent from design for lighting fixtures. We find them with naturalistic and curious animal forms in the metal work which enamored civilized Europe from the late 11th to the 14th Century. This work known as *dinanderie* took its name from a group of metal workers in bronze, copper, and brass in the Netherlands village of Dinant. While *dinanderie* candlesticks are conspicuous among the fixtures used in France, where gilding, *champlevé* and *cloissonné* enameling adorned them, they also reached Italy and Spain. Their vigorous designs, often of animals, are characteristic of late Romanesque sculpture.

The Gothic art influence, so at home in England and France, was never fully domiciled in Italy, whose art had been based on classic models. Still it is common to speak of Italian antiques as Gothic if they have a date prior to the 15th Century and backward to about the middle of the 13th. The fruitfulness of this period, especially in ironwork, has been too long overshadowed by that burst of glory which the Italians themselves call the

Rinascimenta—though the world at large accepts the French term—*Renaissance*. This fact is interesting as evidence of the dominance which France assumed as dictator in matters of art, a dominance from which we emerge only as we inform ourselves more directly from Italy. The architects have never ceased to give the advice: "Go to Italy," and we repeat it. Go to Italy for the beautiful types and ornament of her lighting fixtures, before as well as during the Renaissance.

The art accomplishment of the 13th and 14th Centuries in the period just preceding the Renaissance is increasingly appreciated to-day. It saw the construction of the great palaces and public buildings in Florence and other Tuscan cities of northern Italy, the Palazzo Vecchio in Florence, the Doge's Palace in Venice. Many of the famous houses of the merchants, especially in Tuscany, were built during this period though in the earlier Romanesque style which prevailed in Italian architecture even in the Renaissance. Splendid ironwork in sockets for banners, torches, cressets, and lantern brackets stood out boldly from the house walls. Fine lanterns distinguished the houses of men of civic prominence. Brackets with great rings were placed to hold poles on which to swing superb oriental carpets or figured velvets and other textiles from the upper windows for public celebrations and festivals.

The villas of Tuscany were older than the magnificent Roman villas of the Renaissance. The interiors, though bare from a modern point of view as were all interiors up to the 17th Century, still boasted much color and beauty. They were neither plain nor dull. Oriental textiles and other treasures adorned them, and though simply lighted, the beauty of scant candle-light might fall pleasantly on a wall frescoed with a charming garden scene, on a sumptuous tapestry, or at least a colorful painted linen hanging.

A clear idea of Italian types of fixtures is the best preparation for a study of those of France, Spain, and England. Italy gained and held a position of art authority with the revival of classic art in the 15th Century, and maintains that authority more widely than ever to-day. Wherever there is any pretension to pure beauty of adornment there is a natural return to the classic tradition of the race, notwithstanding periodic attempts to break from tradition and achieve something entirely new. The attempts seem but to illumine the principle underlying classic beauty and give it a new impetus. This tradition has admitted local and period variants of many kinds but happily they are recognizable and classifiable, so that it is not an appalling undertaking to file them away in memory for future reference and delight.

With the Anglo-Saxon, tradition includes of course the Gothic as well as the classic. Though the Gothic is best studied in France, Spain, and England, Italy is not to be neglected, and we wish especially to call attention to the beautiful ironwork of the fixtures of the Gothic period. Italian handling of iron differs from Spanish. There is a lightness to it, a something gay and Italian. Perhaps there is not always that sturdy quality of the metal itself, as in Spain. It may be a bit frivolous, a little too lace-like for iron, but it has its place in the general picture of the pre-Renaissance interior and a pleasing one. So acceptable were these fixtures in the home and the church that the iron-worker was slow in coming under the sway of the Renaissance classic revival. Italian ironwork flourished amazingly, and iron lighting fixtures became so beautified with scroll and floral forms that their popularity extended through the 15th Century. Iron is as closely and typically associated with the Gothic period as bronze is with the Renaissance, although Italian ironwork was notable long before the 13th Century, but it was then wrought with heat and hammer. In the 14th Century iron was used like any other material with file and saw, chisel and vise, bolt and rivet. Sheet iron was cut, pierced, and hammered into flower, leaf, and other forms. The perfected ironwork of the East was brought to Venice by her trading ships so that Venice worked independently and her decorative ironwork was free of French or English influence elsewhere evident.

Candlesticks with a spike or pricket on which to stick the candle first appeared in simple forms, but in the 15th Century Venice made them elaborately with removable branches. The *torciere* for the floor was a simple iron rod set upon three feet, with its top sharpened to a point for the pricket. The *corona*—crown or hoop, was later added to this upright and was supported by more or less ornamental brackets. Later still it surrounded a single candle socket as decoration, not support. Early *coronas* held prickets or sockets for a number of candles. When lighted this gave the effect of a ring of lights which is closely associated with the Gothic interior in other countries, especially in France where it was called the *couronne de lumière*. This form grew more elaborate by the addition of other *coronas*, smaller at top than bottom, forming a cone or pyramid, an effective arrangement of lighted candles. The structure presented many possibilities of adornment. The stem itself was twisted and knopped—knobbed; a 15th Century example shows the knopped stem dividing into two strands only to join again—a nice piece of smithing. The brackets took on various scrolled patterns, the hoops were decorated, and scrolls and flowers sprang from stem and *corona* in highly ornate fashion with clusters of leaves, lilies, and flower spikes.

While the ancient Romans and earlier Etruscans had been wonderful bronze workers, the casting of bronze had been long neglected. In the 13th Century there was a revival, but Gothic design left little impression on bronze work. The fine craftsmanship of Flanders at this time gained it a just fame and the influence of the Flemish school spread widely. There are some very beautiful candlesticks of this period which are classed as Flemish-Italian. They are really works of art, the study of which forms the proper introduction to the more sophisticated Renaissance examples. Some are signed pieces. One pair by Giordans, 14th Century, is typical. The graceful column stems are knopped in the middle and mounted on broadly spreading domed bases, not high like the Venetian and Near Eastern types but low and incurved, spreading even more broadly at bottom, and supported on simple scrolled feet. Bold acanthus scrolling decorates the entire surface. There is a fine border on the central knop. The candle urn has a gadrooned bottom. The proportions show a mastery of both form and ornament.

Other fixtures were made of bronze but they were often Romanesque. Large bronze *candelabri* in the Roman style, imposing *torciere, candelieri,* and *lampade* were found in churches and palaces. The *lucerna* was a survival of the Roman lamp and was fittingly made of bronze. It was a small covered bowl-like receptacle to hold oil on which to float one or more wicks, which protruded from spouts somewhat like a teapot's. There were bronze hand lamps used on tables or pedestals, and lamps with chains to hang from brackets or from the ceiling. For the church there were beautiful votive lamps of bronze or silver; seven-branched candlesticks with the figure of the Virgin; and magnificent *candelabri* for the large Paschal candles from which other candles were lighted in religious ceremonials. The size of church candles grew stupendously and their fixtures with them. The candle in Naples which after six years is still burning *in memoriam* of Caruso has a year longer to burn. Even in England, enormous candles were used in the cathedrals. One at Canterbury in 1457 weighed 300 pounds.

A favorite form of candlestick was that of a human figure bearing a candle-holder of some sort, suggestive of the servant who held the torch at table. For the altar this figure was frequently an angel. Pairs of kneeling figures, like Niccolo Pisano's angel, held large candlesticks, as they did later during the Renaissance. Candlesticks had prickets or sockets. The *padellina, bobèche* or saucer-like member, to catch the drippings, was an early invention.

Hanging lights developed from the small metal ring, which held a light suspended in the Catacombs, to the superb *corona* which attained magnificent proportions.

Lanterns were either a common necessity or an uncommon luxury like those hung at the house door. They were usually of iron, with architectural openings (Fig. II). The typical framework had vertical openings, as large at top as at bottom. This more or less slender framework was finished with a point at top and bottom; often crowned with a coronet of leaves; a leaf rosette finishing it below, usually with a large ring. The entire surface might be covered with simple scrollwork. Twisted bars set like outriders often finished the corners, in the position later occupied by the small turrets in the *torretta* lanterns, as in the Spanish *faroles atorreonados.*

Modern lighting fixtures have so persistently taken their inspiration from Renaissance types that these earlier and rarer
forms have been neglected except by collectors; even our museums
have little to show. Yet among their designs there is a rich choice
of characteristic and beautiful models quite desirable for many
a modern interior.

Before the Renaissance, in the 15th Century, the lighting of
interiors was rarely more than that of bare necessity. With the
Renaissance, types of lighting fixtures became established. The
lighting of interiors began to develop, not as an art in itself,
but it appropriated the full blossoming of Renaissance art forms
and motifs in the making of its fixtures; so that while we have
to-day developed the art of lighting *per se,* we have yet to exceed
the art of the lighting fixture of the Italian Renaissance. A superb
Renaissance griffin, that chimerical winged beast beloved of designers, conceived with a style and dash that rivals the Chinese
dragon at its finest, acts as a bracket to hold a wall-light or from
which to swing a lantern. On the stem of a single candlestick,
even a table candlestick, is found such a wealth of ornamental
detail as literally to form a composite of all the important characteristic art motifs of ancient Rome.

It is difficult for us to conceive the stir and enthusiasm of
the art world upon the bringing to light from the hills of Rome
splendid examples of art and ornament of the ancient Empire.
Excavations of archæological and art treasures are so frequent to-
day and we are so familiar with the works of many periods of
ancient art that it is not easy for us to realize the delight which
these works inspired.

Those were days of dearth in art compared with the reawaken-
ing, literally the "new birth"—*renaissance,* which followed. Brunelleschi, going down to Rome from Florence in 1403 and returning to Florence, with his northern energy spread the new-old
language of classic art, and it ran from mouth to ear, from hand
to eye, throughout Europe. Leonardo da Vinci made an extensive
study of the precious finds and spread the work as far as England.
And when the designers—the artist craftsmen that followed,

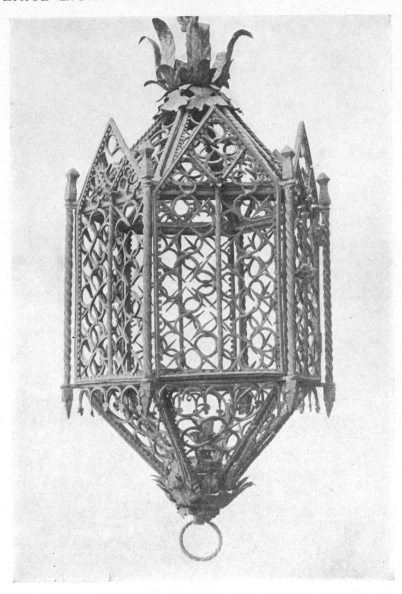

II. A gilded iron Italian lantern of Gothic type made in the late 15th or early
16th Century. Note the fine handling of the quatrefoil motif in the scrollwork,
the architectural window structure, the twisted bars at the corners, the leaf finials.
Courtesy Bagués, Inc.

learned to work in the new-old manner, foreign Dukes, Princes, and Kings summoned them to their Courts to glorify their reigns.

We can form some idea of the power of the classic revival from the virility of its persistence even to our own time. It is astonishing how many of the styles of Renaissance lighting fixtures alone have persisted and served as both model and inspiration for architects and designers, with only occasional intermissions, right down the years to this very day. To Italy we go for source inspiration as to a fountain that has never run dry. As several of the old Roman aqueducts are still pouring their inexhaustible floods of water into the fountains of the Roman city, so Italy's art ideas are continuing to refresh the world from a seemingly inexhaustible reservoir. This fountain reaches far down to the well-spring of Roman works and through them to the original Greek models. It refreshed the French artists and their work blossomed into magnificent, and later into exquisite forms. It stimulated the work of the Spaniard. It slaked the thirst for beauty of the Islanders and gave to Tudor England that profusion of ornament that has set a standard of decoration for the Anglo-Saxon race on both sides of the Atlantic.

The splendid bronze work of the Romans, dug up bit by bit from the ancient hills, inspired Italian workers in metal to renew the ancient achievements in this impressionable medium, and we rejoice to-day in the success of these efforts. But the Italy of their day had seen a millennium pass over its ways and works since classic times, and while ancient Roman craftsmanship was virile and forceful, Italy of the 15th Century added facility, lightness, and a clear perception of beauty which has enriched the world by a multitude of superb art forms. The Roman candelabrum was heavy and sturdy compared with the gracious Renaissance interpretation of the same form (Fig. III). Michael Angelo, Raphael, and other artists of the day made designs for those superb monumental candelabra which still beautify Italy. They not only rivaled the ancient models but added to their adornment the wealth of delicate and graceful art motifs characteristic of the Renaissance.

Remember we are two or three hundred years earlier than the excavating of Herculaneum and Pompeii, which brought to light many exquisitely beautiful lamps and tripods in use in the homes of the 1st Century, and reflecting the combined Greek and Roman culture. But there is still a wealth of design material, that almost bewilders by its profusion, dating from the Renaissance and running well into the 17th Century.

Ironwork came into superb florescence, often polychromed and gilded. Iron torch holders and cressets were still in use. These cressets were bracket-like contrivances designed to hold various kinds of more or less luminous inflammable material. A north Italian 15th Century cresset is as decorative as if it were pure ornament with no practical intent. It springs from the outer house wall with the lively swing of a growing thing, and in fact it is foliated like a lily stalk, swinging upward in a C-curve; the basket tall and splendid posited on the stalk like a great blossom; its high side uprights end in formal fleurs-de-lis; its central pricket overtops the sides like a lily pistil and terminates aloft. When filled with coils of pitch-covered rope, however brilliant or fluctuating the light, the splendor of the cresset itself would stand out boldly. Lanterns were beautifully designed, occasionally with a Saracenic touch suggestive of the tin lantern characteristic of Spain. Brass too embellished the ironwork or was used alone. The hanging sanctuary lamps were often of brass though quite commonly of silver. The extraordinary increase of luxury toward the end of the 16th Century had its final expression in furniture made of silver. So that it was small wonder that silver was not thought too costly for lamps.

Wood was splendidly carved, polychromed, and gilded. The Tuscan walnut candelabra reached magnificent heights (Fig. 1). Venetian wood lanterns of the period are notable, with their elaborate scrollwork and cherubs profusely gilded, but those of the late 16th Century with highly ornate Baroque ornament are even more typically Venetian. Venetian glass was used for candlesticks. Pottery, especially the rich lustered ware of Gubbio, made highly decorative candle-holders. Marble was never more expertly handled nor with more impressive effect than in the monumental

III. This superb 15th Century Italian Renaissance bronze *candelabro torciere* incorporates Renaissance structural and decorative motifs in a masterly way. Courtesy National Museum, Florence, Italy.

candelabra of the Renaissance, covered as they are with superb carvings of acanthus leaf scrolls and other motifs of the period.

Candlesticks were works of art whether for the home or the church, the table or the altar. Table candlesticks were of varying heights from two inches to over three feet. They were made of bronze plain or gilded; of brass; of silver and silver-gilt—covered with gold; of iron, plain, polychromed or gilded; often of wood effectively carved and polychromed, gilded or silvered. They were made of Venetian glass, clear with that quality and greenish hue peculiar to early Venetian work which is never quite clear, colored and joyously so, and gilt. Lustrous pottery too added its beauty to the Renaissance home in the form of maiolica candlesticks, some beautifully painted on the smooth white slip coating which covered this ware, and lustered. There are many types of these smaller candlesticks. The best known is that with a swelling shaft rising from a base with three feet and terminating in a bowl support for the candle the whole profusely ornamented if of bronze or silver (Fig. 2.), generally plain when of brass, and more or less elaborated in wood. Candlesticks often repeat the designs of the large ornamental candelabra—the stem composed of various vase-shaped members, the base a three-sided plinth resting on lion's paw feet, often winged. The design of classic column and base was a natural outcome of the awakened interest in classic models. Another form is of oriental origin especially favored in Venice, always partial to the exotic. Such candlesticks were either made there or produced in the Orient for the Venetian trade. They were low and squat with broad heavy bases expanding in a full reversed or ogee curve. This is a variation of the typical Persian candlestick whose stem rests on a large base like an upturned bowl with straight or curved sides. As in the Near East, such candlesticks were made of metal usually bronze with damascening—following the traditional decoration of the Orient in its fine arabesques. The model with a wide circular base and baluster stem surmounted by moldings was usually decorated with masks, shields, garlands, and interlaced strap-work. One notable example made about 1480 has the design deeply undercut by the artist so that the ornament is pro-

1. A magnificent example of restrained Renaissance design in a 16th Century Florentine *candelabro* of carved and gilded walnut. 1 ft. 5 in. x 5 ft. 3 in. Courtesy French & Co.

duced complete from the wax mold and is untouched by the finishing tool. Such pieces were made by noted artists such as Riccio or
Pollainolo of Padua, for bronze work was the glory of the Renaissance and tempted skilled artists who were really artist-craftsmen.
Figures are prominent in candlestick designs—angels (Fig.

2. *Candeliere d'argento.* An extremely fine 16th Century design in silver-gilt.
7 in. x 18 in. Courtesy French & Co.

3), sirens, *putti* and *amorini*—cherubs and cupids. These appear
either in full figure, or the torsos terminate in beautiful acanthus
scrolling. They hold upright candlesticks or curved cornucopias
for the candles. Cupids on pedestals bear vases with candle sockets. A typical Florentine candlestick of the late 16th Century is
composed of three boys kneeling on a triangular base, and bearing
connected garlands as they uphold a vase-shaped candle socket;

strap-work, masks, and other ornaments adorn the piece. Another favorite design has a mask-adorned vase supported by three boys' figures with dolphins' tails. Still another has a baluster stem on a dome-shaped foot, decorated with pierced and engraved flowers and scrolls. A pair from Venice has a baluster stem with shield, incised ornament, and foliated moldings. Candlesticks of brass were often made in the Venetian manner, engraved and damascened, and modeled along oriental lines, known as bell candlesticks.

3. *Candeliere,* a kneeling figure in polychromed wood in the style of Della Robbia, 16th Century. 23 x 31 in. Modern shade. Courtesy French & Co.

Iron table and floor candlesticks kept their Gothic forms through the 15th Century (Fig. 4). A *torciere di ferro—torchère* of iron, whose tripod feet spread flatly and broadly, low above the floor, with a sharp downward turn and outspreading supports, preserves the vigor of Gothic smithing in the ornamental twists of its stem, its four-sided knop, and its long tapering pricket. An early 16th Century *torchère* has a plain rectangular stem, supporting a saucer-like *bobèche* and an open barred candle socket. The tripod feet spread low but with a subtle S-shaped curve ending

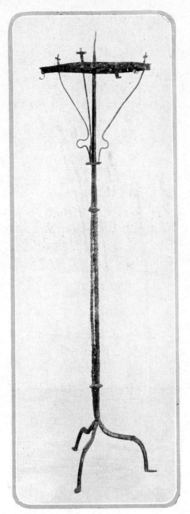

4. This 15th Century iron Gothic *torciere* has its standard divided into two strands and its corona supports embellished with a simple volute. Courtesy French & Co.

in a sharp inward C-curved foot. A 16th Century candlestick has the indented and ornamental crown of Gothic days surrounding its *bobèche,* below which four large leaves bend down to join the stem, the twist in which still shows good smithing; and the four feet shaped like broad upward and incurving leaves proclaim the craftsman's skill. With its original gilding it must have been a splendid piece. But far more sophisticated iron *torchères* were made in the early 16th Century. One from Pistoia terminates in a candle cup—half flower, half urn, on a tall stem springing from a foliage cluster like a lily, the standard ornamented with leaf scrolls and ending in three equally ornate legs. 16th Century work reflects the full beauty of Renaissance design. A *torchère* of wrought-iron ornamented with brass, concentrates all its ornament on the elaborately wrought tripod foot which is almost as complicated with decorative motifs as are the bases of bronze and marble candelabra; the slender shaft rises with small brass knops at intervals, and terminates in an inconspicuous floral *bobèche* and pricket.

Monumental candelabra were made entirely of marble with magnificently ornamented shafts, pedestals, and feet. The typical model of classical origin has a slender vase-shaped or globular stem on a three-sided plinth set up on lion's paw feet. This model was followed with great freedom and originality however and is followed with just as great freedom by architects and fixture designers to-day. The varying height of the base, the proportions of the members of the standard, and the breadth of the *bobèche*, give wide scope for originality as does the ornamenting of the piece. Besides the all-marble candelabra, many were made of bronze with a base of marble or other stone; many were made wholly of bronze; and others of wood, carved, polychromed, and gilded. Some examples in bronze follow the ancient Roman models quite closely, others show a free handling of the type. One from Florence, early 16th Century, is splendidly conceived with a wide-mouthed bowl topping the standard; the standard itself composed of various vase, jar, and knop motifs; the low pedestal slanting outward to the spreading wing-pawed feet; winged cherub heads, winged sphinxes, and other outstanding ornaments add to the effectiveness of the surface decoration of acanthus and other motifs. Wood was commonly used for large candelabra, especially indoors. 15th Century examples are finely carved, polychromed, and gilded, with that perfection of both conception and execution that rejoices the heart. One from the cathedral at Pistoia, made about 1475, follows closely an antique model in its triangular base and the vase motif of its standard, perfecting a gracious and effective composition.

Bracket lights—*braccio*, were numerous, of bronze, brass, iron, or wood in many designs. A human arm carved in wood and poly-chromed might grasp a torch or hold a lantern. Candlesticks and lanterns were upheld on beautifully scrolled supports effectively designed. Iron brackets, stationary or swinging, were ornamented with clusters of lilies and other flowers and their scrolled leaves, gilded and polychromed (Fig. 5).

The Renaissance saw the beginning of a more common use of multiplied candle-light which reached its pinnacle in the chande-liers of the 17th and 18th Centuries. Candles were often arranged in tiers as in the tiered *coronas* of Gothic days. One rather simple 16th Century example (Fig. 6) has three tiers, the largest one be-low, and is decorated somewhat naïvely with simple curls in the Gothic manner.

Lanterns were architectural with window-like openings, charac-teristically ornamented. They were of bronze, iron, or wood; hung from brackets, placed on poles or pedestals, or without pedestals for use in processions. The famous iron lanterns on the Strozzi Palace in Florence are almost too well-known to need description. Their upstanding spikes are recognizable in many a modern de-sign, but we do not always see the adornment of the three crescents on one of them and the fleurs-de-lis on the other. Lan-terns were hung beside the outer doors and in the open arcades adjoining the courtyard. The great gilded lanterns of Venice at this time were hung on stairways and in corridors or on her stately galleys. These imposing galley lanterns are elaborately pierced and embossed, ornamented with borders and figures, leaves and banners. They are made partly of iron, with lead and glass, and sometimes wood. Gilding makes their ornament splendid. Gothic types persisted with their architectural openings, vertically paned; the body of the lantern as big at top as bottom. Finely wrought 15th and 16th Century examples hang from a single bar or chain;

their sides are like cathedral windows, and their quatrefoil scroll-work is resplendent with gilding. Tin lanterns of the period are frequently of Gothic type, also gilded, often hexagonal and decorated with applied motifs of various kinds, perhaps heart-shaped leaves and fleurs-de-lis gilded both for splendor and to prevent rust. They often hang from three chains. Wooden lan-

5. *Braccio fisso,* 16th Century, permanent wall bracket shows the vigor and charm of Italian ironwork in scroll, flower, and leafage; polychromed. 27 x 33 in. Courtesy French & Co.

terns are finely carved as are the candelabra, polychromed and gilded. A hexagonal model might be nicely balanced top and bottom by a hexagonal pyramid continuing the structural form, and crowned by a typical Renaissance jar or vase motif. Bronze naturally went to the making of lanterns modeled on the accepted framework of the period, and enriched by elaborate Renaissance decoration. The characteristic Renaissance lantern is rectangular and slopes to a trim bottom like the street lamp of kerosene days on American lamp posts. This typical framework was used by the craftsmen to build up those incomparably beautiful conceptions which later workers strove to equal.

Lamps were of great elaboration in classic forms—ships, grotesques, satyrs, dragons, sphinxes, animals, shells, eagle's claws, etc. Some were small hand lamps, some placed on uprights a foot or more in height, to set on tables or other articles of furniture. They were of bronze, brass, and glass. Some of the most beautiful

6. *Lumiera* in iron, an early 16th Century example showing the increasing rings for prickets and sockets. 26 in. x 3 ft. Courtesy French & Co.

bronze lamps in the world date from the Renaissance, finely modeled by artists of distinction. The *navicella* or galley was a favorite theme, its sides exquisitely decorated in relief. One late 15th or early 16th Century example is adorned with sea gods and medallions; on the cover Cupid rides triumphantly on a dolphin with foliated fins. A Florentine lamp of the same date and type, and decorated with typical acanthus and scroll ornament, is supported on a baluster stem with three lion's paw feet. Splendid vigorous craftsmanship went to the making of these small pieces.

One from Florence 5¼ in. high is a scallop shell surmounted by a figure of Vulcan with every detail of his trade; dolphin, mask, and wreathage enrich the piece. An early 16th Century lamp from an antique model, has a shell handle set between two dolphins and is finely decorated in relief with tritons and a scene of sacrifice to Hermes. Another is a dragon with a murex shell on the point of its tail, the pedestal ornamented with garlands and terminal figures. Another dragon, from whose mouth issues the flame, has its tail curled back for a handle. Beautifully modeled figures were frequent in lamp designs, some curiously conceived. One is a male winged figure with the lamp's beak protruding from his breast; beneath his cap a loop forms a handle. Another whose design is of antique origin is in the form of a satyr's head mounted on an eagle's claw; his beard and eyebrows foliated in that elaborate scrolled curling peculiar to Renaissance ornament; his mouth is the burner. A Florentine lamp, evidently also from an ancient model, is in the shape of a negro's head on a balustered pillar; lizards crawl around the tripod foot and the pillar is enriched with masks, birds, and other characteristic motifs. Grotesques were not infrequent; one is a horned female sphinx, the lamp nozzle formed by a snail on her breast. A dwarf in a Phrygian cap—the pointed cap like that of our own Goddess of Liberty, clings around the neck of a vine-garlanded ass' head, which forms the lamp. This too is evidently modeled from an older form, probably in terra cotta of which so many old Roman lamps were made. Besides the small hand lamps, the table lamp was widely used. Its type, from an old Roman model, was well established—an oil reservoir set slightly above the middle of a tall rod terminating in a handle. The reservoir was beautifully ornamented in the Renaissance style. Hanging lamps were numerous, the most beautiful ones often for the sanctuary, of silver, bronze, or brass, frequently of enormous weight and size. Their shapes are similar, usually vase-shaped varying from the narrow-necked round-bellied forms to the shallower basins, and often highly ornamented with *amorini* and other Renaissance motifs. Sometimes the bowls were surrounded by branching candle sockets as in the *lampadario*. Silver was the favorite metal as in Spain. But Spain lost her superb silverware by the cart-load when Napoleon became her conqueror and seized it only to destroy it; so that to-day the brass sanctuary lamp is considered typically Spanish while the silver lamp is allotted to Italy. These silver lamps were greatly varied in form and beautifully ornamented in elaborate *repoussé* work. The 16th Century sanctuary lamp presents an important link between the lamp and the chandelier in the design of the *lampadario* with its candle branches. In one example (Fig. IV) and that of silver, the central vase is elongated and elaborated into a form quickly recognizable in the baluster stem of many a later chandelier. From its largest central member, and a smaller one below it, spring two tiers of brackets. These are formed like griffins showing oriental influence, and each bears on its head an urn for a lamp. The three hanging chains are formed of decorative solid ovals linked together, a larger ornamental one midway. Its workmanship is superb. There are many bronze hanging lamps. The one that inspired Galileo with the idea of the pendulum, as he watched it swinging in the Cathedral at Pisa, is an elaborate type of coronet with flying cupids, a theme which many later designers have used to great advantage in their chandeliers.

During the late 16th and the 17th Century, Renaissance types persisted and slowly took on Baroque ornament. This period boasts an extreme richness, including as it does the old Gothic and Renaissance fixtures and adding those of the newer mode. Purists may shrug shoulders at this assembly and caution against a degeneration of the older types. They may insist upon pure Gothic and pure Renaissance, and warn against the mid-16th Century revolt of Michael Angelo which, in weariness of the very perfection of Renaissance art, led him into the riot of the Baroque. But we can enjoy all and choose what we will, and there are many simple as well as resplendent and decorative fixtures classed in this period. For instance we find a 17th Century brass table candlestick, 25½ in. high. It is not of the Renaissance, one can see at a glance, still it has charm. The stem is hexagonal, and the urn and inverted vase members of which it is composed, have

IV. This 16th Century Italian silver *lampadario* illustrates the evolution of the
baluster branched chandelier from the sanctuary lamp. Elaborate *repoussé* ornament; the griffin brackets showing Saracenic influence. Courtesy French & Co.

an over-emphasis—spreading out here and pinching in there, which no earlier designer would have thought of attempting. Still the candlestick has a dash and style that is delightful in such a simple unadorned piece. Even the bold scrolls on the corners of its three-sided plinth and the attenuation of its scrolled feet are in keeping with the general interpretation of the type. As you analyze it, you may feel that it is something like a column of circus acrobats standing one, two, three upon each other's heads, the middle one upside down, but like the poising acrobats who snap into a sudden instant of absolute stillness—motionless, the stem of this big brass candlestick proves its poise. Another example in wood—a floor candelabrum, has this same bravado. The standard is rounded in swelling jar and vase forms cupped in acanthus or gadrooning, with a fully formed *tassa*—cup on stem, for the *bobèche* and socket. Analyze it, and you find nothing that is not of Renaissance type but each member is exaggerated in both form and ornament, even to the scrolls at the corners of the triangular plinth and the lion's paw feet. It is the same with pole lanterns placed on a base, some bases of stone, some of wood. One 17th Century example on a wooden base (Fig. 7) has the original red velvet wrapping the small circular pole of its stem, interrupted a little above midway with a carved and gilded acanthus ornament. There is little in the outline to differentiate it from Renaissance models. It is set a little higher—the proportions are different; but the scrolled feet on the molded plinth are voluptuous, so is the ornament of the lantern itself. It is Baroque, not Renaissance. This same bold swing of independence runs through all the fixtures of this period giving them virility and dash even if they lack the repose of pure Renaissance examples. There is plenty of color and gilding and at last abundance of lustrous glass.

Candlesticks and candelabra were made of many materials: silver, brass, iron, wood, pottery, and glass. Plated silver was used to some extent in candlesticks, candelabra, and hanging lamps. Baluster types of stem were general. Pottery was gayly painted and gilded; sometimes in the form of a kneeling angel bearing a baluster candlestick. Pewter was in use, especially for candlesticks, and for lamps in the Roman style. Magnificent silver candlesticks lighted the salons, and where these were too costly, pewter and brass were substituted in elaborate baluster designs. Tripod floor lights were still made of iron, their ornamentation tending ever to more natural vine and flower forms.

Wall brackets and chandeliers evolved many characteristic types, but others harked back to earlier periods. Much of the iron-work presents that inimitable quality which the French describe as *"du travail soigné."* A 17th Century polychromed iron wall bracket for three lights would never be confused with a Gothic piece; the sophisticated scrolling of the branches, long serrated leaves ornamenting them, the sharp decisive scroll midway, the broad shallow cup of the open flower below the pricket, all bespeak a mastery and deliberation peculiar to the period. It must have been called the "new art" of its day. The really new things how-ever were the fixtures with glass and crystal pendants, which were increasingly used, giving greater brilliancy to 17th and 18th Cen-tury interiors. Sconces and various bracket forms were added to the girandoles and chandeliers—the most characteristic fixtures of the day. Mirror-backed sconces—*specchi colle lumiere,* were etched and decorated in many ways. Italy is credited with the introduction of the *lumiera di cristallo*—the crystal chandelier, as well as the wall sconce, those beautiful fixtures that charmed Amer-ica, France, and England by their lively gayety. While iron and bronze were still used, brass and crystal became the fashion. There were many characteristic types of wall brackets and chandeliers. Crystal and glass pendants constantly multiplied. Small branched chandeliers continued in favor well into the 18th Century. To the full-bodied swelling forms of Baroque ornament, human figures, particularly women's figures, were added. Chandeliers with many candle branches were often decorated with elaborate floral bou-quets. A Venetian chandelier of the late 17th or early 18th Century is of clear glass with pendants and colored glass rosettes or flowers. It is made for twelve candles. Another of the same period has eight sockets. Some were extremely complicated and ornate, made in that style of glass-work most commonly associated with Venice.

7. *Lampione,* a pole lantern of carved and gilded wood with original velvet
on pole. Style of Louis XIV, about 1700. Height 9 ft. 4 in. Courtesy French
& Co.

One gay chandelier has tiny bell-like flowers dangling from its branches, and is topped by a multitude of delicate sprays and finials.

Sumptuous iron lanterns, gilded and polychromed, stood on poles or hung from magnificent brackets. A Venetian gilt lantern of this period still shows that Saracenic influence which continued to enamor Venice, in the long slender proportions of its design, its domed top and pierced metal-work. The domed tops always bespeak the Saracen, as do the corner minarets or turrets, and the pierced metal-work. This work is conspicuous in the tin models and relates them to Spanish work of the same date. Many of them are stunning pieces, from Venice and elsewhere. When mounted on decorative carved and gilded wooden brackets, they appealed especially to the taste of the day. One bracket formed like a human arm holds a lantern high aloft; and capping the stepped dome is a sprightly flag gayly curled as in a spanking breeze. Another, a polychromed scrolled wooden bracket, terminates in three branches each supporting a tall slender painted lantern, the middle one of majestic height. The Saracenic influence is plain in dome and outline, pierced metal, and the diagonal painted striping of the corner supports. An example of the late 17th Century has the bulbous top fashionable at the time, and is capped by an ornamental finial in the shape of a lion holding a floating pennant. Women's figures ornament the corners of the glassed panes. Cupids in the style of the day hold up the lower molding bracing themselves against the lantern's curved bottom. A Venetian lantern of carved wood, gilded and polychromed, is typically of the period with its splurge of Baroque ornament. It is four-sided with grouped *amorini* topping it, while others peer above each corner. Boldly carved acanthus leafage decorates it, and it is finished below by a splendid ornament. Gorgeously scrolled openings for the glass panes belittle the tiny light within. Such lanterns added greatly to the splendor of the City of the Doges at this time and were an important item of furnishing rather than a mere decorative accessory.

Lucerne—lamps on a rod in the old classic form, multiplied.

They were made of bronze, brass, and pewter. Small lamps were made occasionally of glass. Sanctuary lamps were made in the older types but with *repoussé* ornament in the current Baroque style, of silver (Fig. 8), or brass, and occasionally of pierced brass.

By the 18th Century France had established herself as art dictator of such parts of the world as she contacted, though her influence had been felt in Italy as early as the 17th Century. Curiously too, for the Baroque style had its inception and first development in Italy and spread to France only to return, stamped with the approval of Louis XIV and his coterie of artists and with the character of the Louis XIV style. The sumptuous trend of 17th Century fixtures gave way to the greater nicety demanded by later French fashions. But Italy accepted the 18th Century Rococo style of France with a verve peculiarly her own. Venice was especially impressionable and her Rococo fixtures have a charm only recently appraised at their true value. Cosmopolitan, and with her fondness for everything that was brought to her, Venice shows the most delightful variants of the French modes. The Chinese decorative influence which so enamored France, England, and America at this time, found its way into Italy and affected decoration to some extent. Candlesticks and other fixtures made frequent use of figures, which took precedence over other decorative motifs, as in the 17th Century. Candelabra, with wall brackets, and chandeliers increased their branches to meet the requirement for a greater number of candles; and the art of lighting for decorative effect became a prominent factor in house furnishing. Walls were paneled with costly fabrics or painted in imitation of Watteau, so that suitable sconces, girandoles, and chandeliers were required in the French mode, and had to be placed properly both for decoration and illumination. Italy at large retained her older types of fixtures so that big single candlesticks and candelabra were still made, as were the older types of brackets. Wood and other materials were employed. The carved wooden candlesticks and candelabra were not abandoned, but permanent fixtures were increasingly used. The newer types of sconces and even chandeliers were made of tin gayly painted. Brackets in the style of the French *appliques* were brightly ornamented with colored flowers and foliage. These too had several candle branches, frequently five. Venetian mirrors were framed in the styles of Louis XIV and XV with gilded metal candle-holders springing from many of their frames. The fashion of incorporating porcelain figures or groups in the fixtures, as well as porcelain flowers, so exquisitely done in France, was also current

8. A superb 17th Century silver *lampada*—sanctuary lamp. 10 x 26 in. This form was also made much larger. Courtesy French & Co.

in Italy. Capo di Monte, Dresden, and other wares were so used.

A mid-18th Century chandelier of iron (Fig. 9), is wrought lightly and fancifully beyond all hint of the sturdy character of its metal. Its small overhead canopy suggests the *chinoiserie* pagoda. Its scrolled framework is decorated with flowers and leaves naturally colored, and enthroned as in a bower sits a lovely figure of Capo di Monte porcelain. Italy accomplished such things in her own way, quite distinct from the better known French work, and should be given credit for the accomplishment. Candelabra, wall brackets, and chandeliers composed of wrought-iron flowers were typically Venetian. They were decorated with roses, carnations, and daisies with their leaves, and painted naturally or fantas-

9. *Lumiera Capo di Monte*, a delightful Venetian confection, first half of 18th Century, with a *Capo di Monte* porcelain figure embowered in flowers of exquisitely painted tin. 25 x 33 in. Courtesy French & Co.

tically. But iron and tin were not the only metals; *cuivre doré*— gilded copper so popular in France, won fashionable approval though ironwork in the Louis XV style continued, and pervades Italy even today because it still accords with the national predilection. There was a bewildering array of delightful fixtures in glass, as whimsical as soap bubbles and as colorful as nosegays. Candlesticks, candelabra for many lights, and elaborate chandeliers were made at Venice. The gaudy character of some of the chandeliers in colored glass is often deplored, but there are others so delectable as to be ample excuse for unlimited experiment.

One 18th Century Venetian glass candelabrum (Fig. 10 and

10. *Candeliero Veneziano*, a charming 18th Century example of Venetian glass work with beautiful colored flowers. Made in many sections. Height 24 in. Courtesy French & Co.

Frontispiece in colors), made in many sections and put together on a metal frame, is as dignified as nature herself and almost as lovely. Its swirling ornament, garlands, and flower-like *bobèches* are mounted on a tall well-proportioned stem, and the whole presents as charming an appeal as anything ever made by man. Lanterns were fantastic with small outstanding turrets at their corners, or they were star-shaped, domed, pierced, and leaf-adorned, and were profusely gilded. For all their lack of purity of style, occasional examples are both dignified and restrained. One of these is an oblong lantern, with cut corners, set on scrolled feet; entirely of glass with that geometrical complexity which delighted Spain, but without any fussiness to tease the eye. Tassels, which Spain considered an integral part of her lanterns, were accepted in Italy and adorn many other fixtures.

With the unearthing of the household secrets of Herculaneum and Pompeii about the mid-18th Century, a wave of classicism swept for the third time over Italy, but did not produce the splendid results of its 15th Century revival. Quite curiously Italy felt this later revival of neo-classicism by way of France, whose art leadership had been acknowledged for many years; but it seems odd to find works of this period classed as Italian *Louis Seize*. Still her interpretation of this Louis XVI style, of that of the Directoire, and the Empire have a distinctly native flavor which makes them Italian and different. An increasing number of silver candlesticks was used, especially in Venice. A pair in tortose-shell inlaid with etched mother-of-pearl, is part of a toilet-set made about 1780. Silver sconces were placed in the opera boxes of great ladies, and these boxes might be hung with silk, possibly in pale blue and silver. *Cuivre doré* was the accepted material for candelabra, though many were of silver or silver-plated. Lighting fixtures in the neo-classic style were an integral part of the room as in France and England. Piranesi, a Venetian, published his monumental and standard works between the years of 1741 and 1769. With the publication of his drawings of classic antiques, their details became familiar to designers. He was an important factor, perhaps the most important native influence, in forming the decorative style of his period. The Directoire and Empire styles in France, based upon the classic, were sponsored by Percier and Fontaine under Napoleon's patronage at the very end of the 18th Century and the early 19th Century. The Empire style was happily domiciled in Italy and the Italian interpretation ranks next to the French.

CHAPTER II

SPAIN

Spain is a country that tempts us to go back and ever back into her past. Her customs, and the things she finds needful for everyday use, have changed so little for hundreds of years that we can readily visualize her earlier periods. Even an expatriated Spaniard will start dreaming, though with open eyes, at the very word *candil*. It may bring to remembrance a homelike kitchen in the very heart of Spain, with his grandmother bending over her cooking examining it intently by the faint light of her own great-great-grandmother's *candil*, just as women have done in Spain for half a millennium at least, perhaps a whole one. For oil of a sort, and the lamp have always supplied Spain's ordinary lighting requirements.

Lighting the old Spanish house was as simple a matter as it is to-day. Torch holders, candlesticks for floor or table, hand lamps, hanging lamps, hanging rings—coronas, for candles, and lanterns were all that early Spain required. These were usually of iron and made with that splendid mastery typical of Spanish ironwork for generations. The more pretentious houses had large brass lamps hung on chains, and crowns of light in the form of a ring or hoop to hold a number of candles. But few houses had all these. The table candlestick, the hand lamp, and the lantern were generally sufficient as they are to-day throughout Spain.

It is difficult to trace just how far back into antiquity goes the humble *palmatoria*, a small candlestick to carry in the hand, as the name naïvely informs us, and the still more humble *candil*. To-day many a Spanish student learns his English hopefully by the light of his *palmatoria*—the invariable student's light; and the affairs of many a household are successfully conducted *in toto* by the light of a small oil *candil*.

34

The word itself provokes memories. A certain street in Seville is called *calle del Candilejo* from "the old woman of the *candil*," who long years ago heard a scuffling and came peering out the window with her *candil* whose faint rays lit on the murder of Peter the Cruel, that terrible king who prowled by night incognito. He met the fate he deserved, although the murderer was recognized and punished because of the old woman's *candil*.

So much for the *candil*, a sort of pan usually of iron with a long handle springing straight up in the air, often turned over so as to hook here and there for convenience. It is sometimes enclosed lantern-like with a shade of pierced metal, iron for the stable but generally of brass when found in the house.

The period styles in Spain are as distinct as those of Italy, France, and England, but they are less familiar and less generally understood. They are clearly enough defined but the difficulty is that they overlap to an astonishing extent. Not even the Orient presents more anomalies in this respect. The conservatism of Spanish thought is extraordinary. The lack of trade intercourse in the interior even to-day is astonishing. The fact that Spain never had a great metropolis like Rome, Paris, or London to dictate its styles is notable. All of these facts account very largely for the condition of the masses of the population. It is a stern barren country despite its inviting promise of "sunny Spain." Through the limitations and barriers of this sternness and barrenness there has burst forth at intervals a certain joyous and exuberant expression resulting in the three florescent period styles—the *Gotico-florido*, the *Plateresco*, and the *Churrigueresco*. It is well to classify the periods by their Spanish names which are both illuminating and explanatory. These periods and styles ought to be better known and need to be known for the intelligent placing and designing of Spanish lighting fixtures.

To run over them briefly we find—

Hispano-Arabe—Spanish-Arabian or Moorish (710–1609)
Romanico or *Romanesco*—Romanesque (11th–15th Century)
Gótico—Gothic (1250–1500)

Mudéjar—Moorish-Gothic, *Hispano-Moresco* or Hispano-
    Moresque (1250–1609)
Gótico-florido—Flowery or Flamboyant Gothic (1492–1700)
Renacimiento—Renaissance (1500–1600)
Mudéjar—Moorish-Renaissance (1500–1610)
El estilo plateresco—Plateresque style (1500–1556)
El estilo desornamentado or *el estilo Herrera*—style of Her-
    rera (1556–1600)
Barroco—Baroque (1600–1715)
Churrigueresco—at height in 1650
French Styles in Spain (18th–19th Century)
    Rococo
    Neo-Classic
    Directoire
    Empire

The Moors were in Spain for nearly a thousand years—about
nine hundred in fact, so that they deeply impressed Spain with
their Saracenic designs, their characteristic use of colors, and their
methods of craftsmanship. But this was in southern and central
Spain, for they occupied, as early as the year 910, all of what is
now Portugal and the southern half of Spain. Northern Spain was
distinct and was more closely allied with France. Northeastern
Spain, the Province of Barcelona with its leading city of the same
name, turned its face eastward and looked to Italy. This seems
rather complicated but clears up as we follow the sequence of
the style influences in the different periods from century to century.

Moorish design was in its glory in the middle of the 8th Century. While the rest of western Europe was in a state of somno-
lence, living in quite primitive fashion, the Moorish Caliphate at
Cordova enjoyed a high state of civilization. The Caliphs drew
about them skilled craftsmen of many sorts, the metal workers
not the least important, and these included the makers of lamps.
During the Moorish period (710–1609) were built the Alhambraic
palaces, about 1250, those superb masterpieces of art and craft

that never cease to fascinate and to provoke wonder. Standing in the great Hall of the Ambassadors in the Alhambra, on the exact square space where stood the throne of Ferdinand and Isabella when Columbus made his memorable appeal to them, we gain a vivid impression of the strength of the Moor, his power and dominion; a dominion it took the Spaniards many centuries to supplant. But we gain a still more vivid impression of his love of beautiful ornament when we examine enraptured the delicacy of the carved and colored plaster work in the Generalife or the Alcazar, and the lustrous tiles in all the palaces. We must remember, especially in the examination of any lighting fixture which may be classed as Moorish or Saracenic, that Persia, farther east by many leagues, had a hand in the lovely arabesques we call Saracenic, and that Persian workmen it is now understood actually worked on the Moorish palaces of the Mohammedans in Spain, as they did later on the incomparable Taj Mahal in India. Where-ever we find the beauty of the arabesque, whether in China, Syria, Asia Minor, Italy, France, England, or Spain we must credit it to Persians and not to the Arabs for whom it was named *arab*esque in ignorance of its origin. This is important to note in examining the pierced and engraved Moorish metal-work of Span-ish fixtures. In the Moorish period, exquisite and fantastic hang-ing lamps were made of pierced brass, bronze, and silver. There was considerable variety in their designs. The superb example in the National Museum at Madrid is the most familiar type. It was made at Granada during the reign of Mohammed III in 1305 and hangs the magnificent length of over seven feet. Turn it upside down, in imagination, and you get the characteristic outline of the Italian Renaissance lantern, for it tapers toward the top in-stead of toward the bottom. It is pierced in an allover arabesque design, the workmanship suggestive of that of Damascus, widely known for its damascened ornament. The openwork design per-mitted the play of fantastic bits of lamplight and shadow to fall upon the beauty of colored plaster work carved in low relief, on lustered tiles, on the soft bloom of oriental rugs and silken cush-ions; while a perfume burner in the shape of a ball with equally

fine pierced design, rolled for *divertissement* on the pavement.
To the Saracen, living in warm climates, this whimsical play of
soft light and shadow through the pierced metal-work of a lamp
is perhaps what the flicker of an open fire is to the northerner.
It has its own charm; but only when the light within is subdued,
and translucent shadows merge without too great abruptness. The
Chinese carried the same idea a step further in their more subtle
use of translucent porcelain especially in the Ch'ien Lung period,
with their pierced barrel-shaped hexagonal lanterns, so precious
to-day we should fear to put the tiniest light inside. While it is
difficult to locate authentic examples of these old Moorish lamps,
the type persists in the Near East, from Egypt all the way around
that end of the Mediterranean to Constantinople, and offers many
possibilities to modern designers. The ideas they incorporate have
not been widely used although the small egg-shaped glass candle
cups almost cry aloud for electric light bulbs. The Spaniards themselves later made successful adaptations of this model, surrounding the lantern-like body with short outstanding candle branches
with sockets. Although the Moors were confined to their kingdom
of Granada in 1200, by the efforts of the Christians, they were not
expelled politically until 1492 by Ferdinand, and the final evacua-
tion did not occur until 1609. Even so, there was a remnant which
adopted Christianity at least nominally and remained to carry on
the effective style of work known as *Mudéjar.*

In the *Romanico* period (11th–15th Century), the Romanesque
art impulse came over the Pyrenees from France. Barcelona had
a notable school of Romanesque sculpture in the 12th Century.
In this period there came into Spain, but sparingly perhaps, those
interesting *dinanderie* candlesticks of decorated metal which the
merchants of the Middle Ages carried far and wide along the
travel-lines of Europe. Though of Romanesque type, in the shape
of animals, grotesques, and other forms, and often decorated with
colored *champelevé* and *cloisonné* enameling, these too suggest
a Near Eastern inspiration. We know that this ware reached Spain,
but not to what extent it found a place in Spanish homes. Romanesque influence spread gradually southward. In 1085 Toledo was

captured from the Moors and came under the influence of the French Romanesque until the mid-13th Century. This period was prolific of superb wrought ironwork. The three European countries to which we look for the finest use of metals in lighting fixtures, each brought a single material to its highest development along with its other accomplishments. Italy used bronze to the *n*th degree in the Renaissance. France perfected gilded metal in her *bronze* and *cuivre doré* and her *ormolu* in the 18th Century. But Spain had done about everything that could be done with wrought-iron before the 15th Century. Although the grill work in her Renaissance *rejas* is her chief glory, scarcely less skill went into the making of lighting fixtures of the Romanesque and Gothic periods, especially the Romanesque. The work shows the mark of the hammer and the iron is always frankly used. Many examples of this work are in the Museum at Barcelona and deserve study.

Candeleros—candlesticks, and *candelabros*—candelabra, were profusely decorated with lilies skillfully and well wrought, simple and conventional. Such fixtures were typical of the 11th, 12th, and 13th Centuries. In the candlesticks, practical use was made of a large grease pan, circular, rectangular, or oval like a plateau set well off the table on simple feet which flattened broadly. These pans were variously edged. A circular one might be turned down in a scalloped frill (Fig. 11), decorated with simple embossing. A rectangular one (Fig. 11) might be fenced about with decorative edging, the top cut in stepped pyramids. From this broad grease pan would spring several candle branches, usually a central upright surrounded by lower prickets or sockets. The arrangement is suggestive of the fine pieces, really *objets d'art,* with which the Romans accommodated their lamps: a statue or group would accompany a standard from which to swing small lamps, the whole conception placed on an ample platform or plateau. The villas of the Roman Governor and his followers in Spain evidently had such lamps for some have been excavated, though it is scarcely probable but possible that the idea survived to this Romanesque period, in which it was again used however primitively. There are other types of candlesticks in which the tall central candle pricket

passed through a ring supported from the base by three or more
uprights. This structure is purely ornamental, reaching about half
way up the standard, sometimes higher, and occasionally star-like
flowers are attached to it by way of ornament. Other examples
add a fancy crown some distance above this structure.

Candelabros attained majestic heights in the 11th Century,

11. Primitive types of *candelabros* in the Catalan style of wrought iron from
Barcelona, 11th Century. Courtesy Arxiv "Mas," Barcelona, Spain.

particularly in north Spain. Catalan up near the Pyrenees developed a certain malleable process in iron working and her smiths
were famous for their native ability. Their work was purely Spanish without any foreign influence. So skilled were Catalan iron-
workers that two of them, Blay and Suñol, were called to Paris to
work on Notre Dame; and even to-day a fine kind of iron is made
by what is called the Catalan process. The *candelabros* are doubtless the most beautiful of these iron fixtures. They are for the
floor, really *torchères*, and local ingenuity has gone far to ornament them attractively. The lily is the favorite motif and it rises

singly or in clusters on tall vigorous stems, from the juncture of the tripod feet. Sometimes lower stalks surround it, springing up from each foot of the tripod or from the central stalk itself. The flower pistils are the candle prickets.

Hanging fixtures were of the same type though often quite primitive. A 13th Century *corona de luz*—crown of light (Fig.

12. Conventionalized lilies terminate the cross strap-work below the flat ring in this 13th Century *corona de luz* of wrought-iron from Barcelona. Courtesy Arxiv "Mas," Barcelona, Spain.

12), made of flat strap-iron has a large outer ring with seven candle sockets and grease pans. It is supported by a cross-bracing upon which is placed a smaller circle holding four similar sockets. The ends of the cross-beams turn upward and terminate in conventional fleurs-de-lis. The corona is suspended by four chains.

The interiors in which these fixtures were placed were dull and barren unless hung with magnificent textiles and these were rare. The heavy rectangular type of furniture common to the Middle Ages was sparsely used even in the castles, those forbidding castles of granite or brick built by the feudal lords of Castile and Aragon, and guarded from their corner watch towers alert for an enemy. Even the beds were metal, made of iron or bronze until the 14th Century. Though Aragon's greatest prosperity was achieved in the 14th Century and the unguarded *palacio* began to replace the *castillo*—or defensive dwelling, in northern and central Spain; still until this movement became general in the 15th Century, the contrast between living conditions in northern and southern Spain was very great. In the north, Spain was fighting for mere existence while the Moors in the south sat on gay silken cushions and rolled their perfumed pierced metal balls on the pavement; the fresh water from the small fountains bubbling up and flowing through the courtyard to cool the house so that intellectual pursuits could be carried on in comfort. The University at Cordova had long rivaled that at Bagdad and Moorish Spain had almost become effete.

The *Gótico* period (1250–1500) is closely associated with that wave of ecclesiastical building in the Gothic style which swept over Spain in grateful appreciation for the triumph of Christianity over Mohammedanism when the Moors were expelled from Granada in 1492. It is an important epoch in the transformation of the Spanish house and its lighting fixtures. Spain had been in a state of war for hundreds of years, and with peace the *hidalgos* were able to leave the *castillos* of their isolated domains in northern and central Spain, and build themselves more gracious dwellings in the *palacios* of the larger cities.

The late arrival of the period styles in Spain brought the Gothic to its height in the 15th Century at a time when Italy had already enjoyed a hundred years of her splendid Renaissance. It seems incredible considering the short separation between Barcelona and Genoa either by land or water, and can be accounted for only by Spanish conservatism and proud self-sufficiency. In an effort to please their conquerors, the Moorish craftsmen, who had a fine knowledge of Gothic detail as well as a mastery of the Moorish, developed the *Hispano-Moresco* style. It is a mingling of Gothic elements with the Arabic—Saracenic, an art originally derived from Greek, Roman, Coptic, and Persian sources. The exquisite craftsmanship of the *Mudéjars* is the special achievement of Spain. It was during this period also that Spain arrived at the pinnacle of her own greatest decorative accomplishment in her unsurpassed ironwork which is distinctly Spanish. Its designs made free use of religious emblems—the elaborately indented crown, the lily, the dove, as well as mythical forms like the *dragón* and *griffo*—griffin. The lighting fixtures were of unsurpassed variety, including earlier forms and accomplishing them with greater elaboration of characteristic ornament. Gothic ornament became extremely florid toward the end of this period, and while it was often highly decorative much of the dignity of the *Gótico* was overshadowed by exuberance. An unrestrained use of such ornament resulted in the *Flamboyant* or *Gótico-florido* (1492-1700), which followed upon the expulsion of the Moors and lasted well into the Renaissance.

Ironwork flourished, the French influence evident as in other Spanish handicrafts. Spain's kings sent over the Pyrenees to France for their queens and these queens brought French styles into favor. About the mid-13th Century the Spanish iron-workers set themselves to outdo the Frenchmen. Such work was not characteristic of the metal itself as in former days but, like bronze and the precious metals, it was chiseled, pierced, embossed in *repoussé* ornament and gilded until it astonished by its very audacity and delighted by its beauty. More varied and fantastic forms were produced in lighting fixtures than in the *Romanesco* period. Later, in the 15th Century, the French style of working iron was blended with the Saracenic of the *Mudéjars;* and finally flowered into the *Gótico-florido*. There were many whimsical and some extremely beautiful *candelabros* in this period. The 14th Century was rich in both types and designs. Feet were usually tripod—the most prac-

tical arrangement. They were made with or without extra under-
bracing, and their variety and character are remarkable. Some
tripods run high up on the standard, some flatten and spread
broadly near the floor. Some have a sort of auxiliary tripod inside a tall slender outer tripod. Some have multiple supports, possibly ten or more. They can be best classified by their heads. Some
for a large single candle have a large grease pan below the socket;
the pan supported by brackets variously shaped. The most characteristic brackets are those which point or pinch outward in the
middle, the point often embellished with a trefoil or a daisy-like
flower. Another type is the *corona de luz* with its ring of lights.
The crowns are either plain edged or indented in various patterns
on one or both edges and pierced in typical Gothic ornament.
There may be one or more coronas on a single *candelabro*. Occasionally the large grease pan is placed beneath a corona and
made large enough to catch the drippings from all its candles.
The *candelabro formando lirios* has a riot of lilies springing up
naturally from shaft and base or rising in three tiers as in some
14th Century examples. This floral ornament is handled quite differently from that of Romanesque days which is more simple and
formal, while the Gothic lilies are more naturalistic. Often the
candle pricket was the pistil of the lily in both periods. The
dragón, a fetching little animal very simply formed, ornaments
much Gothic ironwork. With its fierce gaping and threatening
jaws, it is full of animation and character. The corona appeared
prominently in both standing and hanging fixtures.

The hanging lights suspended by chains were made in many designs. To the elaborate three-tiered coronas might be added a
mosque-like dome of openwork iron supports, suggestive of the
domed pavilion topping the Moorish hanging lamps. These fixtures take on an even greater complication in the *araña Catalana*
of the 14th Century, really an elaborate chandelier. In the middle
of the suspending rod in one example, the supports form a crown
above a bowl ornamented with applied flowers; and below this is
a scalloped arrangement of the flat supports from which spring
the candle branches with sockets and scalloped grease pans; but

most delightful of all is the winged griffin which tops the piece and gives it its unmistakable Spanish character.

The 15th Century added volutes or extra curves with more sophistication to the tripod feet. These volutes or loop motifs are often very finely designed and effective, though in poorer examples they are crude. The *candelabro multiple,* with many prickets arranged perhaps on the two upper sides of a triangle set up like a pyramid, is often well decorated with finely scrolled ornament.

Gothic character was still evident in the magnificent *candelabro de corona de luz* with its elaborate leafage, splendid pierced crowns, fine scrolls, and *griffos* with menacing jaws and sometimes with gnashing teeth and spiked tails. We find plenty of griffins in Italian ornament, but the Spanish griffin is especially naïve, vivacious, and entertaining, accomplished in iron with a kindergarten simplicity.

The corona or crown-form was in quite general use throughout western Europe in the Middle Ages, whenever a large number of lights was required in great halls and in churches. There are notable examples of hanging coronas in France, England, and Germany. That at Aix-la-Chapelle, where Charles V of Spain was crowned Emperor in 1520, is famous. We are reminded how closely this Charles links Spain with Flanders, for he was born in Ghent in 1500 and came to the throne in 1515. But this is taking us into the 16th Century when Flemish bronze chandeliers must have been well known at least in the Court of Spain if not throughout the country.

In the *gran candelabro*—the great candelabrum, we begin to see a transition between the Gothic and Renaissance types. The standard takes on a column-like form, even rectangular in some cases.

Then came the *Renacimiento*—the Renaissance itself (1500–1600). This is Spain's age of splendor. The fruits of conquest and trade permitted luxury and culture, and a positive lust for luxury brought the highly ornamental Renaissance style quickly into vogue during the reign of Charles V. The inland provinces so long isolated began to prosper. Feudalism was abolished and more and more the *hidalgos* left their ancestral estates and built palaces in the cities in the Renaissance style, a style of architecture fashionable well into the 18th Century. The interiors during this Renaissance period were either Italian or combined Italian, Gothic, and *Mudéjar* elements. Spain's interpretation of the Italian Renaissance is the most striking, vigorous, and local of any of the national variants, and differs sharply in its own two distinct interpretations: the *Plateresco* (1500–1550) and *Herrera* (1556–1600) styles.

Zuñiga, a 17th Century Sevillian annalyst, coined the term *plateresco* in his reference to the minute elaboration of the deliberately under-scaled Renaissance architectural ornament as *"fantasias platerescas."* The *platero* was the silversmith. Renaissance silverware was enormously abundant and highly ornate, a sort of luxurious splurge in metal. Salamanca was the most Renaissance in its building of any of the Spanish cities, for it was the home of great patrician families like the Fonsecas, who were to Spain in a way what the de Medici were to Italy. Castilian palaces emphasized stone carving though they contained the inimitable decorative carpentry of *Mudéjar* craftsmen. The Andalusian house of southern Spain was the type built in her colonies and the most familiar one in America.

It is of some importance to visualize these distinctive interiors in order to understand the correct use of the lighting fixtures of this period. When we recall that the glory of the Spanish Renaissance house or palace was its *artesonado,* that superb masterpiece of a ceiling, and the *yeseria*—carved plaster work on walls, or outlining door and window openings; and know the complicated beauty of this *Mudéjar* decoration; we can understand that elaborately designed fixtures were a necessity in the decorative whole. Wrested from the magnificence of this minute splendor of *entourage,* we cannot judge them fairly. Where such superb work was not found, sumptuous Cordova leather, on which gold replaced the earlier silver, formed a wondrous background when covering the walls and hanging the doorways, or even when used for counterpanes, bed hangings, and cushions. The *plateresco* candelabra for floor or table were none too decorative in such a *milieu*, especially with the other furnishings of the day. They followed Italian types but in a Spanish way.

In any country an imported foreign style is interpreted in a national manner; and it is just this interpretation, with its unexpected and individual variants, that is most interesting in Spain's lighting fixtures. Whether from the northern Goths, from the Italians farther east, from the Moors during their occupancy, or finally from France as she assumed the rôle of fashion dictator, each of Spain's period styles is distinctly Spanish. In a sense they are provincial. Even in the Renaissance during her world-wide supremacy, Spain never achieved a great metropolis and was willing to follow the lead of the fashionable world rather than attempt to supplant it. We are not surprised therefore to find well-known foreign models in Spanish lighting fixtures but always made in her own way. As in her furniture, the lack of artists and master craftsmen often required a simplifying of ornament which resulted in real dignity and vigor. This is peculiarly true of Renaissance models like the large *candelabros,* which though less ornate are occasionally more dignified than their superlative Italian models. Abundant silver and gold from America so enriched Spain in return for Isabella's jewels that she became the foremost nation in Europe during the 16th Century, and her conscious supremacy is reflected in her striking interpretation of Renaissance and Baroque styles.

In this 16th Century we find the column type in the *columna de candelabro,* the *candelabro de tallo*—stem, and the *candelabro de tallo cilindrico conico.* Crowns of light in the Gothic style persisted in the iron *candelabros* of the Renaissance period, but these often took on an extra ornamental motif above the tripod feet. These motifs are somewhat like vase handles, and the Renaissance vase form also appears in the corona supports. But more purely Italian models were also favored. It is odd to see the metamorphosis from the typical candelabrum of bronze or marble to a similar form in iron but with some marked divergence. Paschal *candelabros* attain majestic height. One of the 16th Century (Fig. 13), eight feet high, is of cast-iron decorated with polychromed

13. A majestic cathedral Paschal *candelabro* 8 ft. high, of polychromed and gilded cast-iron, *repoussé* Renaissance ornament, 16th Century. Courtesy French & Co.

and gilded *repoussé* ornament. Its plinth is rectangular. The jar-like member bulging on the stem is lightened by some open scroll-

work in frank acknowledgment of the character of its material.
The very large grease pan is an astonishing conception though
typical; accomplished with a bravado truly Spanish, its broad

14. A 16th Century Gothic *candelabro* of wrought-iron with two flower-like
grease pans and the double twisted divided standard peculiarly Gothic. 14 in. x
4 ft. 7 in. Courtesy French & Co.

plump gadrooning underneath, and the ornate openwork of its
corona are refreshing in their very boldness. The more simple
wrought-iron *candelabros* of the 16th Century often have a double
twisted standard or divide in two strands both of which are

twisted. One with a divided strand (Fig. 14) has a small *bobèche* like a broad-petaled open flower, but conventionalized, and slightly above the middle of the stem is a similar though larger addition. One with a double stem twisted together (Fig. 15) has

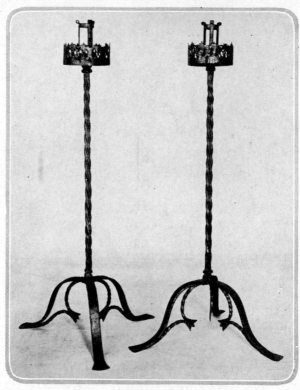

15. This pair of wrought-iron *candelabros*, with twisted standards and pierced crowns, shows the extra inner volutes on the tripods common to later Gothic types, 16th Century, gilded. 21 in. x 3 ft. 8 in. Courtesy French & Co.

extra inner voluted supports on the tripod feet; and an elaborately pierced and indented corona. The coronas of the period are often plain on the top and become an ornamental edging or apron hanging down from the grease pan. A 16th Century version of an earlier Gothic type (Fig. 16), though of wrought-iron, incorporates two slender vase forms in its standard. The tripod feet are simple

and Gothic, but the brackets supporting the grease pan resemble
bronze work. The corona is indented on the bottom edge and its

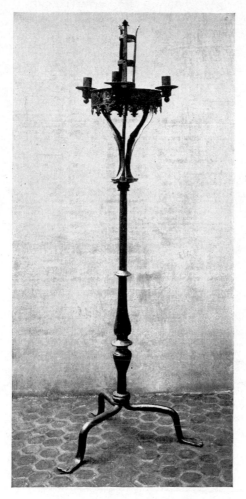

16. A 16th Century version of an earlier Gothic type of wrought-iron *candelabro* with later vase forms introduced in the standard; a crown indented on
lower edge only. Courtesy Hispanic Society of America.

top furnishes a flat support for four candle sockets with *bobèches*,
and also upholds a tall open barred central candle socket. The sup-

ports for the coronas of *candelabros* often assume a vase form
below which is a wide grease pan like a tray or even deeper like a
basin. Pure Gothic forms were also made in this period.

Spanish bronze work followed the Italian mode so that her
bronze *candelabros* are not so typically Spanish as those of iron
or wood. The bronze *candelabros* of the Seville and Burgos cathedrals are notable examples. In many of the designs however there
is less homogeneity than in the Italian. The assembling of various
vase and jar motifs in the standard gives the impression of being
somewhat disjointed because of a certain over-emphasis, while the
outlines of Italian models are fluent and better harmonized.

In wood there are some very interesting examples, of walnut
boldly carved and gilded; some of them even with tripod feet
reminiscent of the Gothic and with a spirally carved standard
equally suggestive. Many of these were originally made with
prickets which were removed in the 18th Century and replaced
by sockets concealed by broad pierced coronas. Some of these are
very broad and highly decorative but their designs proclaim that
they were not born with the piece. Polychroming, so popular in
Italy, was used somewhat in Spain at this time though it did not
displace the Spanish preference for solidly gilded or silvered fixtures especially in iron. A carved walnut *candelabro* of the period
(Fig. 17), both gilded and polychromed, is magnificent. It stands
on a very tall but well proportioned rectangular base ornamented
with carved figures in high relief at each corner, and other figures
set in tall archways on each of its sides. A widely projecting molding finishes the base at top and bottom. The columnar stem is
deeply reeded above a wide band of carved figures like a proces-
sion at its base. Though topped with one of those 18th Century
metal coronas, the piece is splendid and gives an impressive dignity
not to be denied.

Hanging lights were of both iron and bronze; the *lampara*—a
branched chandelier, often had two tiers. Flanders was famous
for her bronze and iron chandeliers in this century, and they
doubtless reached Spain because of the political unity of the two
countries. Venice was making beautiful glass chandeliers at this

time, often with two tiers of lights, and we hear of their reaching Spain in the 17th Century. *Lamparas* of wood, or of wood with iron

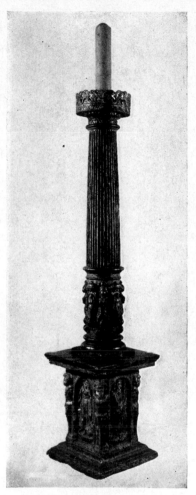

17. This superb 16th Century Paschal *candelabro* is of walnut characteristically carved, polychromed, and gilded. The gilded metal crown is doubtless an 18th Century addition. Courtesy French & Co.

branches in one or two tiers with as many as a dozen branches, were made in the 16th Century but came into more frequent use later. Wood was both silvered and gilded.

Silver sanctuary lamps of the period have disappeared with the other elaborate and massive silverware which Napoleon seized and converted into bullion. Brass lamps similar in type to the Italian, in bowl forms more or less shallow, with suspending chains are more common in 17th and 18th Century examples.

The *velon*—the lamp of Roman type, similar to the Italian *lucerna,* set on a tall upright rod was made of iron exquisitely fashioned. Glass lamps were produced at Barcelona but these were in the Venetian mode. Spanish glass has a bold character that distinguishes it, and is often decorated with that wavy milk-white line so frequently used to ornament ancient Roman glass. Glass lamps were plain or colored, often pale amber and designed in the Roman fashion.

Renaissance ironwork in *el estilo plateresco* is worked as finely as precious metal, with gold leaf beaten in or gold applied in liquid form. Color is rarely found except on the candelabra in the Italian mode, for the Spaniards used color on iron only when needed in heraldic ornament, though they were profuse in their use of gold especially in the Renaissance.

The *Herrera* style (1556–1600), named from the architect, a pupil of Michael Angelo, seems to have left little impression upon lighting fixtures except to encourage plainer forms. It is known as *el estilo desornamentado*—literally the style denuded of ornament. In silver-work we find Juan de Arphe, the noted 16th Century silversmith who has been called the Cellini of Spain, substituting the Greco-Roman style for the *plateresco.* He worked mostly for the church in the second half of the Century, making altar and processional candlesticks as well as large candelabra for the chapel with three branches and three-sided plinths. His lamps were often simple, sometimes rich. Designs for these fixtures remain so that their character may be visualized. The altar candelabra have extraordinary grease pans and are varied in design to accord with the architectural surroundings and the sculptured ornament. Sanctuary lamps were beautifully fashioned and must have been glorious sights amid their Renaissance surroundings. Even the brass sanctuary lamps of the 17th Century, which the world to-day considers typically Spanish, give some idea of the decorative quality of their outlines, if not of their ornament and the play of light upon this queen of metals.

Silver was lavishly used. The sister of Philip II had a silver balustrade weighing 121 pounds placed around her bed, and most of her kitchen utensils were of silver. There was much splendid silverware in the houses of the Spanish grandees because, with the enormous influx of precious metal from America, silversmiths flocked to Spain from France, Italy, and Germany. When the French looted the Escorial Palace in 1810, they despoiled it of the largest number of silver and gold objects then in Europe, among them many lamps. They filled ten camp wagons from the Escorial alone. From one cathedral they took five tons of old silverware. Since Spain's loss of so much of her plate, her brass sanctuary lamps have acquired an unusual importance. They follow Italian models pretty closely but with less ornament.

With the 17th and 18th Centuries, we come to what the connoisseurs consider a decline in the styles of almost every country, but these centuries enriched the world with three distinct period styles. Two of them, the Baroque and Neo-classic, had their inception in Italy but, with the Rococo, all three were dominated by France as she arose to a position of world power. Spain's supremacy was weakened and finally crashed having no sure foundation.

Following the severe and gloomy reign of Philip II, during which his sycophants did what they could to strip the gladness of beauty from the land, there burst forth the *Barroco*—Baroque (1600–1750), a great resurgence of splendor in ornament glittering with gold and riotous with color. In the most extravagant epoch of this Baroque period the *Churrigueresco* style (1650) of the Salamanca architect Churrigura, came into favor, but concurrently Spain lost her world power with her naval defeats, and with the loss of prestige there was little left but bombast.

Her styles lost distinction. Still Spain's interpretation of the Baroque is so assertive that it has become representative of all Spain and all periods to those unacquainted with the sequence and provenance of her decorative styles. The *Barroco* was particularly at home in Andalusia, traditionally accustomed to abundant ornament. The bold characteristic carving was gilded and accompanied with strong coloring in red, blue, and gold. With the disappearance of the beautiful carved plaster work of the Moors in Andalusia, walls were covered with fabrics. Cushions and low stools; lacquered furniture in green, ivory white, and red, preferably red; gilding; and inlaying with ivory, tortoise-shell, ebony, bronze, and silver; highly ornate braziers of copper or solid silver; rich upholstery in leather, quilted fabrics, velvets, and especially figured stuffs; brass nail-heads; and rich gold embroidered brocades; to these add the colorful East Indian palampores, and the demand for lighting fixtures in keeping with such an assemblage will be evident. But this was in Andalusia. Northern Spain clung to older ways and its own provincial furnishings. But Mexico fell under the sway of the *Churrigueresco* to such an extent that she built a $2,000,000 church in Oaxaca, and palaces in the same style.

The iron *candelabro arquitectural* of the 17th Century is lithe and gracious in outline with its vase-like members and shows none of the *Barroco* influence, but other *candelabros* (Fig. 18) and *lamparas* especially in other materials, were conceived with that riot of decoration which usually comes to mind when the average person thinks of anything Spanish. Bronze, brass, tin, copper, silver, wood, and glass went into their making, as well as iron which was never abandoned. Wood is especially adapted to the display of carved and gilded Baroque ornament and was much used for *candelabros,* carved with heavy scrolling, cartouches, and cherubs, and set up on paw feet. Candlesticks were upheld by kneeling figures in the Italian manner.

The chandelier received attention and was developed in the current fashions. Those of carved and gilded wood were made in one or two tiers. Flanders and Italy, and then France set the styles; but the chandelier never achieved the place in the Spanish home that it did elsewhere. The beauty of the pierced metal hanging lamp of the Moors pervaded Spain, as a dream sifts through the active thought of a wide-awake day, and the Spanish lantern never fully gave way to the chandelier. Brass sanctuary lamps had many interesting variations of form and ornament, keeping the general bowl or basin shape, often ornamented with outstanding widely spaced scrolled motifs, reminiscent of ironwork. Capped by a dome or canopy and hung by ornamental chains—these chains suggesting

18. A late 17th or early 18th Century pair of iron *candelabros* with the elaborate decoration of the *Barroco*. The stems are brass knobbed, and the iron polychromed. Courtesy French & Co.

the lantern form, the outline of the Moorish mosque lamp was thus never lost; and the beauty of its pierced ornament was preserved in the elaborate openwork designs of the links and sometimes the additional draped chains. These lamps are usually larger than the Italian of the same type. They are ordinarily about 18 to 24 inches in diameter while the Italian are about 12 to 16. The Italian are more delicate than the Spanish with lighter chains. These Spanish brass lamps were quite abundant in the late 17th and early 18th Centuries.

The table lamp in the shape of the *velon* became sophisticated in both iron and brass; decorated with broad gadrooning; the handle, topping the rod, of elaborate design; and with large eye-shades of the same metals in the form of shells upheld by cupids. This kind of decoration is peculiarly Spanish. The shell is the emblem of Spain's patron saint San Diego—St. James, and appears constantly in decoration as do the crown and lily, emblems of the Virgin. These motifs were still used on lighting fixtures for the home as well as the church for they were still similar.

Glass was made into lamps but never took the place of metal, although the Barcelona glass-workers followed Venetian models but these were more for ornament than use and were far from ordinary. The famous crystal chandelier in the Escorial was of 17th Century Italian make.

The Spanish *Barroco* with its deep shadows and high lights, a style peculiarly expressive of the deep and sudden contrasts of Spain, persisted in its 17th Century manner well into the 18th Century, when the main streams of the Rococo, the Neo-classic, the Directoire and in the 19th Century the Empire trickled in as they did, but never overwhelmingly. Spain was still conservative and when she lost her grandeur she clung more tenaciously to her provincial and local furnishings. Possibly she reverted to older types, lacking incentive for progress. She did not attempt to stem the tide of French fashions though she echoed them somewhat feebly.

With the 18th Century, Spain came under the general influences common to other European countries, but her interpretation of these types is still bold and outstanding. The finesse of the Moorish touch and the minutia of the *plateresco* had long been lost to her. She handled her materials with less delicacy and this heavier touch in the French forms gives a severity and assertiveness peculiarly Spanish. The same materials went into the making of fix-

tures as in the 17th Century except that bronze, *ormolu,* and brass
were found most suitable for the Rococo types and those which

19. An 18th Century *candelabro* of wrought-iron with finials and knobs of
brass. Its crown, formed like a flower, is a later addition. Courtesy French & Co.

followed. Ironwork at length lost its distinctive character (Fig.
19) except when it repeated the older and primitive models. Elaborate hanging lamps were still made for the sanctuary but usu-

20. This large sanctuary lamp shows the ornate character of 18th Century design in its openwork and scrolled ornaments. Courtesy French & Co.

ally of brass (Fig. 20). One in the Seville Cathedral preserves the old corona motif, but three flying cupids labor to uphold it though it hangs from stout chains, those elaborate chains to which Spain still clung as a last evidence of her love of the pierced openwork designs of the Moors.

As in France and Italy, glass was in vogue and many beautiful chandeliers, as well as splendid candlesticks, lovely girandoles, and *appliques* were made or imported in the late 18th Century. Some were made in the Venetian manner with colored flowers and leaves, but far from showing the exquisite touch of Venetian work. Others were of clear glass with various types of pendants. The Catalan and Maiorcan glass-workers ever attempted to rival the Venetians, and interesting glass chandeliers illumined Spanish and Maiorcan homes. They have the same baluster stems fashionable in Italy and France, the same bouquet motif spraying from the top, not a little suggestive of older ironwork designs, though the gracious curving of the candle arms and the brilliant glass pendants are a far cry from primitive Spain. It had already been proved in the last Century that a glass or crystal chandelier could be as happily domiciled in a Spanish palace as could a pierced Moorish lamp, an interesting fact in interior decoration. The chandeliers which adorned the homes of the rich and the great however were far from equaling the brilliant complexity of such Italian work as that of the 17th Century chandelier in the Escorial with its multitude of pendants and garlands and even elaborately constructed peacocks. But chandeliers, girandoles, and *appliques* were only for the ultrafashionable, a small world in Spain, and she is far from giving up even to-day her *palmatoria* and her *candil.*

CHAPTER III

SPAIN—LANTERNS

THE Spanish lantern won for itself much consideration and an important place in Spanish life both inside the house and out. This conquest was not confined to Spain for it has spread far westward to Florida, around the Mexican Gulf, and up the California coast. Here Spain herself took a stand in the 16th Century and held her ground, though barely held it, during the centuries which followed until the complete absorption of her territory—through purchase or otherwise, by the United States. But she gained a firmer foothold than she knew, though not the kind she sought. The few examples of her buildings, widely isolated except in Mexico, have some of them stood to this day. Their peculiar suitability to the climate of the localities in which they were built has been accepted with approval and become a standard all the way around our wide sweeping shore-line to south and west. And because this shore-line has now become the winter playground of our whole country, building in the Spanish and allied styles has spread abroad a multitude of homes, many for year-round living, all of which may be suitably accommodated with half a dozen or so good Spanish lanterns. Occasional use is also found for them throughout the country, wherever Spanish or Italian furnishings make them acceptable.

This sudden upspringing of interest in things Spanish has combed Spain to a nicety of almost everything superfluous, and there never was much superfluity in Spain, so that great collections of furnishings have poured through the New York art auction rooms, the antique shops, and the hands of interior decorators. We have witnessed this continuing siege of a vast army of Spanish lanterns from its first scant vanguard until it has seemed to grow to abnormal proportions and to isolate itself from everything of its kind. The Spanish lantern has temporarily overshadowed the Italian, the French, and the Saracenic to all of which it paid tribute—in fact owed its very existence. In this motley array of lanterns, mostly 17th and 18th Century examples with a few from the 19th, Andalusia is almost exclusively represented.

Now Andalusia is far from being the whole of Spain, and the Andalusian lantern is not the only lantern that is Spanish. But so large did the trade in ornamental tin lanterns become in the 18th Century in southern and central Spain, especially Toledo, that when one speaks of a Spanish lantern instantly there comes to mind some intriguing example of that skilled combination of glass and gilded tin in complicated geometrical arrangement, typically Andalusian.

It took many centuries to unite Spain politically, and even to this day each different province clings to its own distinct customs and inherited household effects; so that a complete résumé of Spanish lanterns would take us into byways of provincial types almost too numerous to classify. When the Spaniards finally pushed the Moors off their peninsula into Africa, they had a big work before them in settling the large Moorish territory formerly ruled by the Caliphs; territory gradually narrowed to a small plot with the fortress city of Granada as its stronghold. There was constant fighting from century to century. But when Granada fell in 1492, peace came at last to the whole country.

We can glimpse something of the welcome peace of those days, when we visualize the slow-moving ox carts which met the silver boat from America at Guadalquivir, fifty miles from Seville, and carried its ingots in quiet safety to that city; for fierce *hidalgos* and desperate Moors had ceased their depredations. It is in Seville that the most persistent use of beautiful lanterns continues to this day.

The *conquistadores*, those natives of Estremadura adjoining Portugal, had gone forth and conquered Mexico and Peru from whence sailed the silver boats, and had returned to build their own dreams of home into severe stone with interiors both austere and comfortless however stored with treasure. Between these austere dwellings and the gracious interiors farther east there is little analogy, and their lighting fixtures witness the fact. In the north iron was dominant. In the south it was not thought suitable for indoor use by well-to-do Spaniards until the 15th Century, that is, after the Moors had withdrawn; for the Moors worked exquisitely in the more subtle metals like bronze. Spanish ideas of luxury as a whole however were influenced to a great extent by those of the Moors who like other orientals inclined to precious metals, or bronze damascened with precious metals in elaborate ornament. Spaniards made good use of the *Mudéjar* skilled metal workers while they remained in Spain, and this fact is evident in lantern making.

The distinction between a hanging lamp and a lantern is not always closely drawn. The pierced hanging lamp of the Moors, made of bronze, brass, or silver, when wholly enclosed is really a lantern. These lamps were glassless. Although glass was known in Spain when it was a Roman province, we hear little of it until the 15th Century, and the Moors seem to have had little use for it.

In following lantern making through the Spanish periods, it is interesting to find that the outline of the Moorish pierced metal hanging lamp, which is domed at top and slopes gradually outward to a rounded base, does not again recur in lanterns though the hanging sanctuary lamp retains it. If you follow with your eye its four chains suspended from a small canopy to the basin below (Fig. 20), you will find that they outline the four sides of the typical mosque lamp, really a lantern, which the Moors covered completely with pierced metal. The outline of the Gothic lantern was equilateral, with vertical panes. The Renaissance lantern was the mosque lamp turned upside down. These three outlines classify the lantern pretty definitely as to type if not in period, for all types overlap.

Lanterns as part of the builder's work, go far back into the Gothic and Romanesque periods. Where there was no street or highway lighting, lanterns at the house door were indispensable if that door were at all pretentious, particularly if it were of a civil character. Lanterns for domestic use in the *patio*, vestibule, or hall were even more of a necessity and were found in cottage and palace alike. The *candil* was easily converted into a lantern by adding a protecting sheet of pierced metal. In fact such lanterns were used in stable and kitchen very anciently. Lantern making as an art in itself starts with the 16th Century which means the Gothic period in Spain with the Renaissance influence spreading slowly from Italy.

Ironwork was at its height; so was silversmithing. Glass was made in some abundance in Barcelona and Toledo. Brass work was a Mohammedan heritage. Bronze work though largely in the Italian style had a hint of the Moorish tradition. Silver and goldsmith's work of the period are little more than memories, having gone into Napoleon's melting pot. This leaves brass and bronze, beloved of the Moors; iron, Spain's glory; and finally tin as the metals which framed her splendid and often fantastic glass conceptions, those *faroles* still so cherished that they are found in every house in Seville. Indoors they now often hang from single heavy red silk cords or stand on red poles. The old pole lantern, used to light the way at night or in processions, is now often mounted on a base of marble or other stone. Hanging lanterns sometimes swing from metal brackets, and flat-bottom lanterns are placed on tables.

The period styles associated with Spanish lanterns of the 16th, 17th, and 18th Centuries are the *Gótico, Mudéjar, Renacimiento,* and *Barroco* or *estilo Churrigueresco.* All of these styles may be found in the later lanterns as curiously combined as in a picture puzzle. There is one fine quality which Spanish lanterns possess whenever *Mudéjar* influence is evident. However debased the design, however finicky the ornament, if the top or bottom is finished by a curved outlining as of a Moorish dome, the modeling of this dome is exquisite because inherent and traditional with its workman. It may be the only really beautiful element in an otherwise ugly lantern. East is East and its very persistence assures beauty. Saracenic decorative influence is often found in Sicily and Italy, and it is sometimes prominent in an Early Italian lantern. But Italy always had Saracenic art second-hand, or through occasional imported workers. The Saracens, in this case the Moors, were actually on Spanish soil, and as long as any of them remained their inherited craftsmanship and design were in evidence.

Three points are prominent in the designs of Spanish lanterns: their architectural character, the lily, and the crown. Their window-like openings, when of any architectural pretension, are apt to be Moorish; either a single or triple arch or the favorite Moorish window—the *ajimez*, a double arch divided by a single slender column.

Another Moorish element is the subtly beautiful double or S-curve of the mosque dome, found in both the tops and bottoms of lanterns, and occasionally at top and bottom of the projecting *torreones*—turrets, placed at the angles of the *faroles atorreonados* —or turret lanterns. The domed outline of the Christian cathedral is not lacking in some models, as well as the lily, emblematic of the Annunciation of the Virgin, and the crown. Another architectural motif is the baluster railing, reminiscent of the Spanish balcony; while most characteristically Spanish are the *torreones* which persisted almost to the point of absurdity in some late 18th Century models.

In decoration, the glass-work is apt to be geometrical and Moorish while the metal ornament is the Gothic lily, the *Mudéjar* arabesque, the Renaissance acanthus, and the potted plant of the *patio*. The elaborated tassel, beloved of the Saracens on their horse bridles and accoutrements, adorns all later examples and has become for us, as for Spaniards, a part of them. So established is the tassel habit in Spain that even bed-linen is felt incomplete without its small linen tassels.

As early as the 14th Century some good lanterns were made, as we know from rare examples: one of brass, rectangular, a little higher than square, ornamented in *repoussé* and with large window-like openings on the sides. These openings have the triple arched top of the Moors and the lantern may be classified as Moorish.

El estilo Gótico is evident in the structure and decoration of both iron and tin lanterns, and is especially prominent in the designs of their open scrolled tops. One form is dome-shaped like the domes of strap-iron in the *araña Catalana*. This dome-shaped top of strap metal-work persisted in the lanterns and was sometimes unduly emphasized and top heavy. Even an urn-shaped model of the later Renaissance might be topped by a strapping of greatly elongated leaf forms. The decorative motif of the lily was the characteristic ornament of Spanish lighting fixtures for church or home from the 11th to the 13th Century, during the Romanesque period. In the Gothic period the corona was the most important motif, but the lily was retained. Both of these ornaments are frequent in the later periods.

The metal-work of lantern frames followed the general character of work of the period in form and ornament. Beaten sheets of iron were put together to make the required model. We must not forget that lantern making as an art was developed in the iron lantern, which the enormous use of tin in the 18th and 19th Centuries practically eliminated, and it reached its perfection in the *farolismo* of the 17th Century, when it was at the height of its vogue. The iron was then beaten into thinner sheets capable of more delicate handling in Renaissance applied ornament and even in the pierced decoration of the Moors. The Spaniards themselves consider that the art declined with the 18th Century. This estimate, however, is from the point of view of an iron-loving race. Tin has its own qualities and advocates, and while it cannot rival iron, iron itself is not a substitute for tin.

Mudéjar influence is found in both the metal-work and the geometric treatment of the glass panes. This glass-work through over-elaboration often becomes so intricate as to lose its beauty. Geometrical patterns were superimposed in the center of the panes, being set out on a different level either beveled or sharp edged. The inequality of Spanish glass added to the effectiveness of the lantern. The most attractive Moorish elements are in the metal-work whether pierced or solid; the pierced metal being the most characteristic. Even in the solid work there is that nicety of the molded form, the soft rounding of dome and corner, a suavity truly oriental and always beautiful.

In outline the *Mudéjar* lantern is often immensely superior to other types, its form being its finest quality. It was inspired by the elongated lines of the mosque lamp, and the most beautiful examples are found in this style. They are occasionally so elongated as to require a small lantern to cap the top, the bottom being equally prolonged by receding angles, curves, and a finial. *Mudéjar* work, even in the later styles of the Renaissance and Baroque, shows a feeling for proportion that is especially fine and is its notable characteristic.

In 16th Century work we see the influence of the *Renacimiento* at last penetrating the *Gótico* and *Mudéjar* models and recognize the differences between these types coming from central and northern Spain and the almost pure Moorish lantern of this period from Andalusia in the south. A large iron cathedral lantern, 52 in. high, from Toledo in central Spain, late 16th Century, shows the Gothic style giving way to the Renaissance. It is rectangular, its entire framework pierced, and its ornament is both Gothic and Renaissance. Glass was used more generally in lanterns in this Century.

Other 16th Century examples are also rectangular but with combined *Mudéjar* and Gothic, or *Mudéjar* and Renaissance influences in crowned domed tops and scrolled bottoms. In some examples we see corner outriders in the form of ornamental metal columns embellished with simple conventional flowers and leaves. Hexagonal shapes came into favor.

One of the most beautiful of these *Mudéjar* lanterns of 15th Century type (Fig. 21) though it may have been actually made in the 16th Century, has none of the crudeness of the early Spanish work but bespeaks the cultured accomplishment of the Saracenic metal worker as plainly as if in finely damascened bronze. Its body is hexagonal with long arched openings, the arching softened by vandyking the edge in minute points, and ornamented by three tiny spaced quatrefoils pierced in the metal. At each corner is a half column on a rectangular pedestal, a touch of ornament on the pedestal to relieve its plainness, the column slender and graceful, topped by a capital resembling those of the Alcazar. A mold-

ing is supported by these columns, and above each capital is a
mask which is crested in an outstanding flare above which rises
a long conventionalized leaf ornament in an S-shaped curve, its
tip curving outward. These flaring curves of mask and leaf are

21. This superb gilded tin *final* of the 15th or 16th Century shows Moorish
influence in its beauty of outline and proportion, domed top, and pierced metal-
work. Courtesy Bagués, Inc.

repeated in the small corner ornaments of the frieze or band
incorporated in the S-shaped domed top, and in small awning-like
openings in each of its six sections. These bits of flaring metal
with the six naturalistically wrought tassels depending from the
molding below the body of the lantern, give an astonishing light-

ness to the whole conception. If it were not for the long receding bowl of the bottom, subtly formed and ornamented, the whole effect would be that of a decorative pavilion in an oriental garden. We are reminded of the exquisite Persian miniatures of this and other centuries, wherein some gorgeously clad Shah is refreshing himself in his garden pavilion set amid flowers. The interesting thing about this gilded tin lantern is the simplicity of ornament which however suggests not only a knowledge of that elaborate allover decoration beloved of the Orient where no inch of the surface is devoid of ornament, but also the fine spacing of Persian ornament. Although the pierced design is of the simplest this suggestion is unmistakable. Its maker knew more than he performed, though he has used his tin honestly and done all that he could with it; his was the skill of the artist craftsman performed *con amore*. He could have made a silver lamp to grace a palace. The mingling of Renaissance mask and leaf forms with Gothic ornament and Moorish outline and tassels in so successful a manner, is far from an ordinary accomplishment.

In contrast, another 16th Century hexagonal lantern of polychromed tin (Fig. 22) shows a lack of this fine sense of proportion, although an ingenious arrangement of an upper lantern above the dome, elongates it to a dignified form. Moorish influence is evident in the piercing of its entire framework, no part of which is left solid. The gallery motif, surrounding the body of the lantern, was a favorite decoration of the later centuries. The flower-like spreading of the top ornament suggests the early Gothic ironwork, except it is solidly formed and only slightly indented. The ornament of leaves as pendant on the bottom also suggests the Gothic, although the idea was elaborated in the acanthus leaves of the Renaissance period. The effectiveness of this lantern when lighted can be guessed at; no part of its structure would be dark, for where glass panes are lacking the metal is minutely pierced. After all the proof of the pudding is the eating thereof, and the test of a lantern is its effectiveness when lighted.

In the transition of styles between the 16th and 17th Centuries, late 16th to early 17th, *Mudéjar* elements persist, as do those of the Renaissance period, but occasionally interpreted in a Baroque manner. One example (Fig. 23) of a curious kind which seems to have been popular shows a peculiar mixture of styles. This type usually appears in rather crudely executed work. It is long and

22. Moorish influence is shown in the elongated outline of this *farol*, as in its piercing and dome. Polychromed tin, 16th Century. Courtesy French & Co.

slender in outline, with *Mudéjar* influence evident in the somewhat debased inverted dome-shape of the bottom and the pierced metal four-sided dome of the top. The crown surmounting it is clumsily scrolled with the fullness of Baroque ornament. But the most curious elements are the outriders at the corners of the panes formed of strips of tin curled into a column which is set well out from the body of the lantern and looped back with leaf brackets at top and bottom. Crimped open flowers are placed at intervals upon the frame, giving the impression of some of the cruder iron-work of the Romanesque period.

A more sophisticated example of this type (Fig. 24) substitutes

23. Both *Mudéjar* and Renaissance influences are evident in this 17th Century *farol* made from a 16th Century model. Note the corner metal outriders, floral ornament, pierced dome and crown. Courtesy French & Co.

beautiful scrollwork joined to the body of the lantern, in place of these outstanding columns, but retains the turned back leaves at top and bottom which are highly elaborated in the Baroque manner and spread out so as to decorate the piece very effectively. Renaissance influence is shown in the small lantern set above the larger one. The framework is hexagonal and broader than the early *Mudéjar* types. The pierced metal dome and crown are showy in the Baroque style.

A typical 17th Century example is very finely proportioned and of true art value. Less skillful designers often exaggerated the crown and depreciated the bottom of the lantern, but here a true sense of proportion is observed. It is remarkable that so much elaboration of glass-work should show so little fussiness. The

24. A Baroque *farol*, 17th or 18th Century; solid scrolls take the place of turrets as in some earlier types, but leafage and other ornament are Baroque. Courtesy French & Co.

pierced metal dome and crown are restrained but typically Baroque.

The 17th Century was prolific in lanterns with glass turrets at each of the four, six, or eight corners. The turrets are extremely varied in shape, proportion, and the finish of top and bottom. These *faroles atorreonados* are as characteristic of Spain as her ancient turreted castles. Other styles have varied outlines—urn-shape, oblong, oblong with accentuated dome at top and reversed at bottom, oval, and circular elongated by domed top and shaped finial bottom. Tops are somewhat wide and slope sharply to a small, well formed inconspicuous crown. In some the crown becomes almost negligible, in others the crown and dome overtop too small a lantern. Some tops are of pierced metal, others of openwork strapped metal scrollings.

Renaissance lanterns often merely echo Italian and French forms, but with that simplified quality characteristically Spanish. Even if many sided and globular, made of small panes of glass, they are topped by pierced metal-work typically Spanish, and as often have a solid nicely molded metal bottom reminiscent of the Moors.

Many interesting examples of the *faroles atorreonados* exist in a good state of preservation. The *Mudéjar* influence is still evident although the handling of the design may be Baroque. One of the most perfect in outline, proclaiming the sensitive feeling of the *Mudéjar* for form, is rectangular with its oblong panes of glass set out in a very deep bevel, itself of glass, and has the turreted corners formed of long glass strips terminating at top and bottom with a nicely proportioned cone of pierced metal in conventional design and topped with a tiny nosegay. The well shaped bottom is of solid metal elongated somewhat with one or two extra motifs and hung with a tassel. Its typical Saracenic dome is ornamented in pierced leaf-work and the crown is similarly perforated. The large piercing of this crown in bold leaf ornament classes it in the Baroque period. Such restrained and dignified examples are not typical however of 17th Century work. Exaggeration is shown in almost every element of lantern designs. It may be in the bottom of the piece, which although nicely molded and pierced in open Baroque leaf design, will have a double instead of a single inverted dome. The cone capping to the turrets although tipped by a simple ball may add the extra ornament of several depending leaves. The most marked exaggeration is in the very large leaves which end the turrets, top and bottom, and dominate the dome-shapes of both. These leaves are great sprawling things as far as possible from the beauty of the acanthus leafage which supposedly inspired them. Still when the lantern is lit the general effect is rather splendid, for glass occupies its entire body in large plain panes and narrow stripped turrets, and the tapering dome is solid with little piercing; the cap is a solid scallop-edged crown. But the Baroque style did not always dominate the design, as in this case, often the only evidence of Baroque ornament was in the bold openwork leafage of the crown itself. A rectangular lantern whose outline is flawless, bespeaking the *Mudéjar*, has inconspicuous turrets with pendent lilies below and dear little potted plants above. From the crown springs a beautiful bouquet of natural lilies and buds, and the composition is as charming as anything that could be desired.

Occasionally a 17th Century urn-shaped lantern will be quite sophisticated and very beautiful, suggestive of Italian bronze work, even if of iron or tin, and will more likely be six than four-sided and as a matter of course capped with a metal crown or occasionally an open blossom-like motif. Such lanterns abandon completely all *Mudéjar* elements and show a mingling of the Renaissance and Baroque. One, rectangular with a typical Renaissance outline which tapers downward, has its glass panes in six sections; the top is strapped with beautifully shaped acanthus leafage and capped by a naturalistic regal crown. The bottom is finished with elongated scrolls depending from the framework with a cupped finial of acanthus leaves below and small well shaped leaves running up onto the framework. Similar leaves decorate the upper framing of the sides and above the middle of each pane is an upright oval patera flanked by C-shaped scrolls. This model was frequently used, and slightly varied. The panes were divided into four (Fig. 25) as well as six sections, but the leaf ornaments are apt to be too large and completely dominate the structure. Even in this period when Baroque ornament was uppermost, a hint of the Saracens will occasionally be found in the pierced arabesque dome of a beautiful and highly sophisticated Renaissance urn-shaped lantern, plainly simulating Renaissance bronze work, though ornamented in the Baroque style. Another lantern, as typically Baroque as may be in its bold ornament, and as distinctly Renaissance in its glassed panes, still bespeaks the Moor in the almost exaggerated elongation of its outline. Again, a long rectangular lantern will be all of pierced metal in arabesques suggestive of both Moor and Italian, and such lanterns are very

25. An 18th Century urn-shaped tin *final* in the Renaissance style common to the 17th Century. Courtesy American Art Association.

handsome. The Moorish ornament may appear in the minute design of a pierced banding where the majority of the ornament is Renaissance.

Flat-bottomed lanterns (Fig. V) are common in this late Baroque period, they are set upon feet of various kinds, some of them sufficiently ornamental so that the lantern may be hung as well as stood upon a table. One example, though a rather queer one, has well shaped acanthus leaves at each corner forming prac-

V. A very fine restrained example of Spanish geometrical glass-work in a table lantern made in the 17th or 18th Century. Courtesy French & Co.

tical feet. The body is rectangular in the Renaissance mode and perfectly plain with four simple large glassed panes and straight banded framework, but the top is stupendous and Baroque at its worst. Four elongated and serrated leaves curve in S-shape, and a clumsy bulging S-shape at that, to join a crown that looks like frosting on a wedding-cake. These leaves are rendered entirely unnecessary by the conspicuous and practical framework within their embrace. Other feet on these flat-bottomed lanterns are shaped like cones, point downward or point upward. Others have rounded feet in the form of heavy looped leaves. Another type though less characteristic sets on a well shaped stem properly proportiond to hold the body of the lantern and pierced in a fine latticework design.

These flat-bottomed lanterns are of several types. Some are of the simple Renaissance rectangular type. Others of this type are elaborated in the most complex geometrical glass construction imaginable, including a modified turret at the corners and an indescribable arrangement of the roof. The pierced crown proclaims them Baroque. Other examples are rectangular or hexagonal following the designs of the period but with the lower appendage lacking. The six-sided lanterns were more apt to take on the highly geometrical complication of glass-work which is considered typically Spanish, though Italy had her own share of these models. Such lanterns are often all of glass, bottom, body, and roof. One which we do not hesitate to describe has a terraced roof arranged in three receding terraces, topped by a crown. The top terrace has four small metal ornaments bedecking it, and from the lower molding of the roof is hung a somewhat crude metal festoon falling upon each of the glass panes below. Reminders of the older turrets are found in irregular box-like protuberances projecting from the lower terrace of the roof. These have pyramidal covers topped by long slender lilies of Easter lily type. A really sensible lantern of the late 17th or early 18th Century is decidedly architectural. It is rectangular like a neat little *porte-cochère* with columns at each corner supported on moldings and upholding moldings which in turn uphold four posts connected by a neat balustrade.

But the effect is not as formal as the description might indicate, the four columns bursting midway into Baroque acanthus leafage; the corner posts are tipped with urns of a sort and end with sharp inverted cones as if intended for feet. But to prove their uselessness a beautifully dome-shaped bottom appendage is added in openwork flower and leaf design and a finial ends this with an ornamental tassel for good measure. Within the little fenced balustrade on top is an arched dome similar to that below, and on top of this is a small architectural lantern with little peep holes in its conical roof. The glass panes are arranged in dignified sections, and the whole effect is good.

Spain did not neglect the pole lantern in the 17th Century nor the *torchère* with the lantern top. One pair of such *torchères* (Fig. 26) is composed of an iron standard with those voluted tripods noted in the sophistication of late Gothic ironwork. The lower half of the stem is twisted, the knops ornamenting it of openwork acanthus leafage, the upper portion a simple rod but decorated with a little formal surface ornament. The lanterns are of tin and glass. The body of the lantern rectangular, of Renaissance type; with broad Baroque acanthus leaves depending from below, and similar but larger leaves rising from above and forming an attractive finial. The whole structure is gilded and accordingly splendid. So much for the 17th Century.

In the 18th Century the *estilo Churrigueresco* or Baroque, which enamored Spain, persisted with a sort of violence which was responsible for some very awful things from the point of view of artistic design, though often amusing because of their very childishness. But there were also some fine types which are perhaps the best known and most popular of all Spanish lanterns. Practically all the late 17th Century designs were repeated. Leaf and floral ornaments became more naturalistic, scrolls more plentiful, if often bombastic, and domes and turrets were capped and crowned with bravado. But there were more demure examples, and while a magnificent bouquet of lilies might top a lantern instead of a crown, an exaggerated leafage sprawl over the frame of another, the tiny potted plant like the flower pot in the *patio*

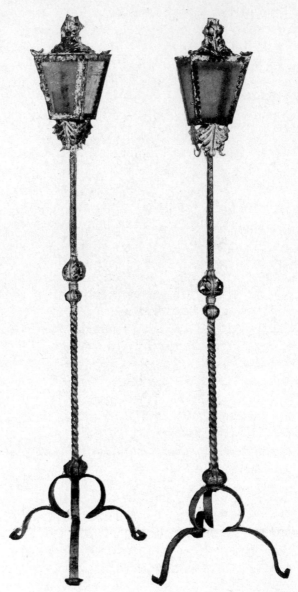

26. A pair of 17th Century tin *faroles* set on iron standards, both gilded. Tripods voluted in late Gothic style. Lanterns urn-shaped and enriched by leaf ornaments. Courtesy French & Co.

continued to hold its place and topped many a turret quite modestly. The bottom was often flat and finished with the same types of feet as in the late 17th Century. Turrets were still in evidence with mosque-like domes and half-domes, giving ample opportunity for pierced ornament; and crowns were never lacking.

27. The top and bottom points of 18th Century glass star *finales* were sometimes elaborated in metal-work. Courtesy American Art Association.

The turret survived in many lanterns merely as a decorative corner motif, barely recognizable. In later examples spikes might rise from these reduced turrets, as overhanging roofs with spiked corners might cap the top of the lantern itself. Colored glass too came into a certain use, and conventional forms like the star-shaped lantern were popular as in Italy. This star design (Fig. 27) was frequently handled very effectively. An eight-pointed star, with a large plain glass octagonal center has an attractive leaf finial on the bottom point, tipped by a tassel; and in place of the top point is a pierced ornamental band, above which is placed a sort of leaf-like canopy which permits the escape of the heat from the light within. Some of these star lanterns have as many as twelve points with elaborate metal framework.

28. A turret lantern with flower pots on the turrets; metal-work of *Mudéjar* type in molded bottom, piercing, and star; Spanish crown top. An 18th Century rendering of a 17th Century type. Courtesy American Art Association.

A turret lantern, with the turrets topped with flower pots was sometimes far from a simple affair in the 18th Century. With a hexagonal body and stepped roof, one example (Fig. 28) is topped by an openwork crown of pontifical type. The side panes are glass as are the turrets, the stepped roof, and the slanting member above the base. In the center of each pane is a circle and within this circle

an eight-pointed star. It would be more attractive to the eye if
the bottom element had been less exaggerated. Its dome-like outline bulges outward as wide as the body of the lantern itself and
then slopes downward by stages to a point which is tassel tipped.
If you turn the illustration upside down you will get an idea of

29. An 18th Century development of a 17th Century model showing *Mudéjar*
and Renaissance influences. Courtesy American Art Association.

what a better craftsman would have done with such an outline, but
it would not have been Spanish.

Sometimes these 18th Century lanterns were perfect gems, beautiful enough to have been fabricated in precious metal instead of
gilded tin. One of these (Fig. 29), a typical 17th Century model
which continued to be made in the 18th Century, is largely Sara-

cenic though there are Spanish and Renaissance additions to its design. Its beautiful slender proportions are Moorish, as are its fine pierced metal bandings and the other pierced metal-work, even though of later design. The detail of the corner turret has been broadened and the side panes reduced and inset. These turrets are roofed with a half-dome of Moorish type but finished with Spanish crowns. The lantern itself has a variant of the Moorish dome and a beautiful pierced metal-work crown in the form of a band slightly flaring and straight edged both top and bottom. The bottom of the lantern also recalls the S-shaped curve of the Moorish dome but with a distinct variation which classes it in this period, and curiously but attractively is finished with a loop made of lovely leaves which are quite foreign to Saracenic design, though they serve to hold the typically Saracenic finish, a highly decorative tassel.

We wish we could illustrate half a hundred of these delightful old lanterns, so constantly do they vary in one way or another. Gilded in the old styles, both for beauty and to prevent oxidization, they were also painted in later days; and when we recall the Spanish vogue for gay colored lacquer furniture in the 17th Century we can appreciate the decorative effect of painted lanterns in the Spanish interior. The *final* is not hung in the center of a room but near the wall or at the end of a hall as its name *final* indicates. The *farol* is a lantern used anywhere.

The great variety of decorative effects, from dignified iron to sprightly tin, is the special value of the Spanish lantern; as practical in a northern dooryard as in a southern *patio*, a royal palace or a humble home. Spain is Spain, and to many a sober grown-up is still the dream-land of "castles in the air." Even a Spanish lantern swinging in our vestibule will start again the dreams of childhood when we were perfectly certain that "over the hill lies Spain."

CHAPTER IV

OLD FRANCE AND LOUIS XIV

ANCIENT France is an ambiguous term, for France was not really France until the 9th Century. Anciently it was Gaul, and Gallic it remains even though many centuries have passed over it, bringing various influences from without. Cæsar wrote in his day: "All Gaul is divided into three parts," and we shall find a tripartite division helpful in considering its lighting fixtures, though not the geographical division made by Cæsar.

In the Middle Ages, Roman and Christian art influences mingled. This Medieval period—the French *Moyen Âge*, including the years from the 5th to the 15th Century, is receiving much more attention artistically than used to be accorded it. The thousand years of the pre-Renaissance era includes, as in Spain and Italy, the Romanesque and Gothic periods and, of almost equal importance to southern France, it includes the sway of the Eastern Roman Empire with its capital at Byzantium, later the city of Constantinople. This Byzantine period (328–1453) was an active one, for Byzantium enjoyed great wealth, culture, and luxury during many centuries. Through her influence the art motifs and the metal-work of Syria and Asia Minor reached Europe, both facts important in the making of lighting fixtures of this time.

The Romanesque period (700–1100) saw the mingling of Christian and Roman art in *le style Roman* or Romanesque, at the time of the world's history which has been commonly called the Dark Ages (5th to 11th Centuries). The *Gothique* period followed (1108–1515). *Le style Gothique*—the Gothic style, held sway until Renaissance influences from Italy in the 16th Century had their fruition in the days of Richelieu during the reign of Louis XIII, and finally resulted in the extraordinary accomplishment of the French Baroque known as *le style Louis Quatorze* in the 17th.

Then France found herself magnificently her own mistress and dictated both styles and manners for the Western World.

But we cannot so lightly step into those gorgeous days of *le grand monarque*. Even in the Dark Ages, the houses in that part of the world had a little oil lamp and perhaps added a little candlestick to the firelight. We can be sure that daylight never sufficed the indefatigable warrior Charlemagne (crowned Emperor in 800 A. D.). Like many another leader of men, his interests were wide and he led in all. After the strenuous activity of the day, he surrounded himself at nightfall with learned men, and discussed with them such subjects as astronomy, music, logic, grammar, literature, and natural history. Books were few and writing the exclusive profession of the scholar, yet Charlemagne himself learned to write, an unusual royal accomplishment for that time.

Early French lighting fixtures were either purely utilitarian or they bore the unmistakable mark of the countries from which they were brought or copied. Here we reach the necessity of noting the three divisions of French territory. Southern France which bordered the Mediterranean had long been familiar with Italy and Byzantium, and traders brought her their foreign wares and ornaments. Little luxury was known in northern France where living was primitive, and such handicraft as existed was of the crudest. Some fine metal-work of their making is known in ornaments for personal adornment but little else. France that bordered the Pyrenees was at one with Spain in the kingdom of Navarre which straddled the mountains. Here were the great iron mines, and here we may expect to find and do still find primitive iron lighting fixtures of the same type on both sides of the Pyrenees. The Spanish *candil* and the French *candile* are similar to this day; both reminiscent of the Roman lamp in the covered types, but as primitive as possible in the uncovered examples—merely a little grease pan with a bent edge to hold the oil and keep the wick out of it, the handle sticking straight up in the air with hook and spike attachment. The spike could be stuck anywhere convenient and the hook hung anywhere a light was habitually needed, thus serving both purposes. Lamps were also permanently suspended, better to light the entire room, as for a celebration when as many as thirty-six might be hung from a single beam of wood or metal. Doubtless this same little oil lamp in France as in Spain was continuously in use from Roman days, as more elaborate examples of the type seem to indicate. Candlesticks were known at least as early as the 8th Century, doubtless earlier, and candelabra in the 11th. This brings us in the late 11th Century, to the interesting time of the *dinanderie* which we also found in Italy and in Spain.

The little Netherlandian village of Dinant had a notable group of workers in bronze, copper, and brass, whose work was conspicuous in Europe until the 14th Century. Candlesticks of their making were in various forms, mostly curious. The low squat types with scrolls, animals' feet, or animals for feet, are as vigorous and active in design as are the squirming dragons, curious quadrupeds, and birds, which either carry human figures holding prickets or have prickets mounted on their own backs. Their vigorous quality is characteristic of late Romanesque sculpture and their workmanship deserves its fame. These chimerical animals became highly sophisticated in the days of *François Premier* but early examples were primitive and crude. Candlesticks were called *chandeliers* and those from Dinant *chandeliers de dinanderie*.

These *chandeliers de dinanderie* furnish an interesting episode in the history of lighting fixtures, linking Europe unmistakably to Asia, both in workmanship and in conception. The Mohammedans of Asia did not all belong to the stricter sect which followed Mohammed's teaching that it was unlawful to have an image of any kind in the house. Those in Spain during the Moorish occupation followed quite strictly the letter of the law, and geometry was carried to its decorative apotheosis in the Moorish Palaces.

But as in Persia, so farther west in Syria and Asia Minor, there were to be found designers and craftsmen who were not so persuaded, or were of other religions; and a beautiful or whimsical thing once made, even though including floral and animal ornament, might be enjoyed by a Mohammedan without danger to his

soul. We find a Saracenic touch in many an animal motif on a
lighting fixture, as the griffins previously noted on the 16th Century silver Italian sanctuary lamp (Fig. IV), where they were
used as brackets. In these *dinanderie* pieces we are often reminded
of a Near Eastern origin although the designs themselves may be
Romanesque. The chimerical animals, serpents, lions, elephants,
and birds; and the decoration of semiprecious stones and enameling, recall Byzantium and the countries farther east. They were
far more exotic in their day than the most whimsical Chinese
objet d'art is in a modern interior, and so delighted Europe that
their vogue lasted many years among the wealthy. There was
plenty of action to interest the eye in a contorted dragon carrying
a human rider who held an enormous open flower, its pistil a
pricket for the candle; the whole forming a practical arrangement,
the flower acting as *bobèche* to catch the candle drippings. Even
when designed as a simple candlestick, the feet have a strident
quality as if they would walk away with the candlestick if it were
not watched. Small candlesticks were constructed of ivory and
other precious materials, with their designs inclining toward fantastic animal forms as in the *dinanderie*. Much ingenious work
was put on the candlesticks of the 12th Century, as England also
bore witness in her famous Gloucester Candlestick (Fig. 69).
12th Century coronas were of silver—gilt and enamel, bronze,
brass, iron, and wood; large and small.

Coronas in the 13th Century were smaller and seldom elaborately made, though occasional votive lamps were quite decorative, one in silver bearing a ship. Previous to the 13th Century
the typical coronas were made of bronze, often *doré*—gilded. The
reign of *St. Louis* (1226–70) saw the height of French ironwork,
which had its own distinctive character as did the Spanish and
Italian. Heavy and massive ornament in all materials was succeeded by a greater freedom and fineness, which was especially
notable in ironwork. Though less vigorous than that of Spain, not
so lace-like as in Italy, it was sprightly, vivacious, and beautiful.
A free use of the lily motif—*lis* or *lys*, was common to all these
countries. There is an increasing tendency to value the artistic

movement which culminated in the 13th Century in its many notable achievements.

So important did the making of lighting fixtures become that there was a corporation, as was the case with so many French handicrafts, for the making of *lampes* and *flambeaux*. A *lampe en couronne* held a number of lights on its *roue de fer*—wheel of iron. Candlesticks were taller than those of the Romanesque period and had one, two, or three knops on their stems; three usually by the end of the 13th Century. Some of these large *torchères* were beautifully wrought in the style of the ironwork of the Gothic period and ornamented with naturalistic flowers and leaves. Set up on tripods with knopped stems, they became highly elaborated in the finer examples though simple for the populace.

The art of the lighting fixture was still in its infancy. The torch, candle, or wick in oil were merely accommodated in a practical or whimsical way. The fixture itself developed in size throughout the *Gothique* period and finally reached what art connoisseurs delight in calling monumentality, in the great Gothic crowns of light. This *couronne de lumière*—the glory of the *Gothique* period, was fitted for lamps or candles and usually hung from three chains. With lamps—small oil cups—*godets,* and called a *lampier,* it gave little light; with multiplied candle-light it was brilliant, and when doubled or tripled in diminishing rings or hexagons as on hanging or floor lights, it produced what was thought in that day to be a marvelous cone of flame.

Hanging coronas were of wood, bronze, copper, silver, or silvergilt; sometimes elaborately decorated in enamel, ivory, rockcrystal, and coral. They were made of *bronze doré*—gilt bronze, before the 13th Century but were later made of *fer forgé*—wroughtiron, during France's period of splendid *Gothique* ironwork. The skilled use of bronze preceded iron, as in Italy and Spain, but more closely, and followed it even more permanently. The large coronas of Rheims and Aix-la-Chapelle were world famous. Iron coronas were not so large, and in the 14th and 15th Centuries were lobed.

Candlesticks were *chandeliers à point* or *à broche*—pricket, or *à bobèche*—socket or nozzle, with or without a grease pan; with solid base or with feet; taller, and with knobbed stems they were ingeniously made in openwork bronze, iron, silver, ivory, enamel, rock-crystal, and gold. In the 15th Century the *tige à bague*—ringed stem, came into vogue. *Bobèche* then designated the socket with or without a grease pan, and a *chandelier* designated any candle fixture until the 18th Century, as the candle itself was a *chandelle* in French. Candlesticks were of iron for the kitchen, of decorated wood for the great hall, of bronze or copper for other rooms in fine houses, and brass in the cottage, a distinction common until the 17th Century.

Dinanderie and work done in a similar style were in vogue, so was *champelevé* enamel—that is, colored enamels set in designs gouged out of the metal, as in the *chandeliers Limousins* of Limoges, about twelve to eighteen inches in height. Enameled candlesticks of the 13th Century were famous. *Bougeoirs*—little flat candlesticks, the *bougie* was another name for a candle, were called *pallete, esconce, cresset, mestier;* some burned perfumes, a Gothic habit of luxury as it was a Saracenic; some were protected lantern-like to carry through corridors or across the court-yard like the *esconce.* A *chandelier mobile* was a small movable or hand candlestick as the name indicates; and the *porte lumière* was any portable light. *Chandeliers de voyage* were demountable for packing and journeying with one's effects from castle to castle, as well as for the use of a traveler; for the *haute monde* changed its residences at different seasons as in Elizabethan England. These *chandeliers de voyage* were made with tall vicious looking prickets set directly on a low base, often polygonal and ornamented with enameling in characteristic designs. *Torchères* made with the same end in view were *flambeaux à pied tournant.*

Bougeoirs à douilles, with sockets, often had a pierced instead of solid socket in the 14th Century. *Chandeliers à pommes* with knopped ornaments or *pommes; chandeliers à fleurs*—with flowers, usually lilies or roses, enameled and gilt; *chandeliers à person-nages*—made in the form of human figures or persons, were the favored types. Low candlesticks for the table were called *chande-liers bassets,* made with a *broche*—a spit or pricket, placed directly on a round or polygonal base, so inconvenient that in the 14th and 15th Centuries the modern type of stem candlestick evolved, with a foot, stem, and *bobèche*. Many of these were made of silver. The word *bobèche* is commonly used to-day for the grease pan but it should be remembered that an earlier use of the word confined it to the socket. Candlesticks came into quite common use in the 14th Century.

The *chandeliers à personnages* are artistic conceptions, as they were in Italy. These early examples are forerunners of the more plentiful work of the 16th Century. The wearisome service of holding torches or candles at the tables of the great or for ceremonious functions was supplanted in the 14th Century by these figures of servants holding one or two candles. They were made of bronze, sometimes of silver. Cellini's famous silver *candélabre Jupitre* was a notable Renaissance example made for *François Premier*.

The types of fixtures were fairly well standardized in the 15th Century. Prickets were still used for candles, but sockets more commonly. Candlesticks were sometimes quite low and formed like a bundle of reeds, called *chandeliers à lobes*—lobed candlesticks (Fig. 30), also in use in the 16th and 17th Centuries. This was a very convenient arrangement as candles of varying sizes could be accommodated and still be held firm and upright. These candlesticks were occasionally made of pottery, but usually of metal ornamented in *repoussé*, or enamel like those from Limoges. Their form suggests bunches of candles or of reeds bound together as in the ancient torch.

Hand candlesticks of bronze were of several types, both pricket and socket. Some were set upon three feet, some had a heavy solid bowl-like base reminiscent of Venetian and Near Eastern models, except that the base was proportionally smaller and the candle stem elaborately ringed instead of tubular. *Flambeaux* were larger than the ordinary candles at this time, and had special fixtures. The Gothic use of this term should not be confused with its later use designating the candlestick. It was much later that they were made small enough to fit an ordinary candle socket.

The *chandelier à bortrole* had a socket that was not of solid metal but pierced, usually with two large openings convenient for removing the remains of a burnt candle. They were of several types, some of them with a heavy inverted bowl base showing again the influence of the Near East. One of these has a stem which ends in a pricket, and bears two closely set candle brackets besides. Another similar model with an ornamental animal in place of a pricket, has two adjustable side brackets on its screw stem,

30. This *chandelier à lobes* of Limoges enamel, exquisitely painted, are signed inside "Noel Loudin" (1585–1681). Courtesy The Anderson Galleries.

upon which they move up and down at a touch. Such candlesticks were sometimes made of silver. Simple models were for a single candle, but still retained a large conspicuous base. Brass candlesticks were in somewhat common use. Traveling candlesticks were made for one or more lights, of silver and other metals. Pricket candlesticks were of iron, copper, bronze, and sometimes of silver or gold. Their designs grew quite complicated. The *bobèche* might be large and bowl-like, ringed or plain sided, and often edged in square battlements, lineal descendants of the vigorous flower forms of the *dinanderie*. One with a large battlemented *bobèche* has a high stepped base, proportionately large. Others have the rings on their stems widened excessively, and bear an extremely large bowl-shaped *bobèche*. One is simple and slender with a graceful stem incorporating a vase form, forerunner of the popular

Renaissance model. Some have no grease pan but a simple pierced socket, tending toward the jar form used in later periods.

The *flambeau* or torch, was placed in the *torsièr—torchère,* for use in large rooms. These *torsièrs* with crowns are the *couronnes de lumières pédiculées,* that is, with a stem on feet. Their crowns were round or hexagonal and held both sockets and prickets. The elaborate examples when lighted presented that effect of a flaming cone so decorative in the hanging lights. The *candélabre* was in form of a tree or *arbre,* for ecclesiastical uses, or a simple tripod like the *torsièr.* It might have one, two, or three coronas, either round or hexagonal, attached to its stem by cross-bars. They were made in many types and in many materials, sometimes sumptuously ornamented in enamel, gold, and silver, or made of copper or iron.

Chandeliers d'applique were candle brackets for the wall. They came into use in the 14th Century and became one of the most important means of lighting the house in the later periods. The French paid special attention to the artistic development of the wall bracket. Even in Gothic days it was not neglected. They were of iron, occasionally of enamel, gilt or silver; and had both fixed and movable branches. The 14th Century saw a general decline in French ironwork though much of it was still made in good taste.

Lanternes—lanterns, were made for hand use, to be hung, or carried in processions. They were of iron, bronze, or precious metals, often architecturalized in the Gothic manner. Hand lanterns were simple and commonly cylindrical. Those of precious metals might be set with little pieces of glass which was rare at this time. The more beautiful of these lanterns were burned all night especially in bedrooms. Perfumes were sometimes burned in lanterns and perfumed candles were used on festive occasions.

A model characteristically rendered in iron (Fig. 31) was common to the 15th and 16th Centuries, carefully worked out in the structural details of Gothic architecture. It is rectangular. Gothic columns and arches frame the large side openings. Moldings finish it above and below. The bottom ends in a four-sided point

with a sharp in-curve, a simple nicely molded finial and a very
large twisted ring; this twist, in frank admission of the iron of
which it is made, finishes the top and bottom molding and decorates the four rods set as outriders the entire length of each corner,
ending in large rings below and long out curving spikes above.
The top strapping slopes to a pyramid, crested by a double crown.

31. Gothic wrought-iron *lanterne*, 15th or 16th Century, highly architectural
with twisted corner rods and spikes reminiscent of turrets; surmounted by a
crown and lilies suggesting Italy. Courtesy Bagués, Inc.

Each side has a triangular cresting with foliated edge, a foliated
trefoil at the point, and within it is a sharply defined triangle
inclosing a conventional trefoil. The less formal edging of the
four crests is further emphasized by lilies on long stalks which
spring up naturally, reminiscent of the bouquets which topped
many earlier *torchères* and hanging fixtures, as they did so many
18th Century chandeliers.

German mounted animal horns (Fig. 32) accommodating iron

candle brackets were popular in the 14th and 15th Centuries in
northern France, and were used in Germany until the 18th Century.
These fixtures from Germany were more curious than beautiful.
They were suspended by ornamental chains leading to the tips of

32. Animal horns with polychromed wooden figures from Germany were much
in vogue in the Louis XIII period. Wired for electricity. Courtesy Bagués, Inc.

the horns and their juncture. This point of juncture was variously
ornamented, usually with a figure in carved wood which was
painted in various colors; or it might be more fantastically
wrought with castles, scenes, and figures. The horns of deer and
other animals, might accommodate several sets of candle branches,
eight being not uncommon. These hanging lights were much in

vogue in the *Louis Treize*—Louis XIII, period which takes us into the Baroque. 14th and 15th Century hanging chandeliers were of the branched type with six or eight candle branches often decorated with elaborate Gothic foliage. One example incorporates a gallant horseman in its design. They were made of silver, iron, brass, copper, and wood decorated in azure, rose, and gold. 15th Century types were more complicated with their branches in one or more tiers. Copper and bronze were preferred to iron, and silver was used for the sanctuary.

Hanging lamps were of various metals, sometimes a primitive conception in iron, though often more elaborate in silver, silver-gilt, and bronze. Little lamps were shaped to fit into candle sockets.

In the 15th Century torches were still held by servants on festive occasions, as they were as late as the Louis XIV period. Iron floor tripods (Fig. 33) with coronas—*couronnes de lumières pédiculées*, were smaller but set on a tripod as formerly. They were made with one, two, or three coronas attached to the standard by cross-bars. As in Spain there was much ingenuity exhibited in the designs of their supporting brackets. A large grease pan was often placed below these supports. The coronas themselves ranged from plain hoops to elaborately pierced crowns, circular or hexagonal. Iron was not conspicuous in the hanging chandeliers of the period, for the chandelier was given greater consideration especially from the point of view of the material used. Each material dictated its form and ornament, a factor which was neglected in the 17th and 18th Centuries when all materials took on the form and ornament of the successive period styles, often belying their innate character and wresting it away from its natural limitations. 15th Century hanging lights were frequently of the cross-bar type —*croisée de bois*, of wood. Some were elaborated with carving and wrought ironwork in handsomely scrolled candle branches. Copper and bronze were also in use, branched with ornate foliage and scrolled designs in one or two tiers. Some were gilded and painted in azure and rose.

Wall brackets made practical use of reflectors to increase the

light, placed so as to add to the general lighting of the room. They
were made for as many as three candles. Lamps received increased
attention. Some were of iron, some of silver. The *candile* persisted.
The *chandelier à huile* was a small lamp fitted into the socket of

33. Splendid spread of tripod feet in a 15th Century *torsièr* of wrought-iron.
Courtesy Arnold, Seligmann, Rey & Co.

a candlestick, sometimes permanently soldered. They were of
bronze and other metals but less ornate than other *chandeliers*.
They were often similar to earlier models, and were sometimes
known as *chandeliers façon d'Allemagne*—candlesticks made in
the German style.

Several of the greatest French artists were influenced by the Italian revival of classic art as early as 1450. An added impulse was given this interest when Charles VIII conquered Naples in 1495, and a few years later another impetus was received when Louis XII defeated the Milanese. Charles VIII brought both Italian artists and works of art to France, and quite an immigration of Italian artists followed in the reign of Louis XII attracted by the large sums of money offered them by the French nobility. This movement culminated under Francis I (1515–47) who was a devoted patron of Renaissance art. He was contemporary with Henry VIII of England and Charles V of Spain. It is an interesting fact that not only national pride but the personal rivalry of these monarchs increased the demand for novel and splendid art accomplishment which drew heavily upon the arts of southern Europe to add to the prestige of their Courts. The splendor exhibited at the meeting of Francis and Henry at The Field of the Cloth of Gold has long stood as a symbol of their times. The lighting fixtures which decorated the pavilions in which Francis displayed his wealth were many of them silver. There were twenty silver sconces in the banquet hall. Ten were silver-gilt and each held five candles.

Such consummate Italian artists as Leonardo da Vinci and Benvenuto Cellini were tempted to the Court of Francis I. The two Italian queens, Catherine—granddaughter of Lorenzo de Medici and wife of Henry II of France (1547–59), besides Marie —wife of Henry IV (1589–1610), had not a little to do with the further popularizing of furnishings in the Italian style.

The reign of Francis I marks a transition in which Renaissance influences mingled with the Gothic. His interest lay chiefly in the Province of Touraine about one hundred and fifty miles southeast of Paris. He added a wing to the Castle of *Blois,* built the *Château* at *Chambord,* started *Chenonceaux,* built a portion of *Fontainebleau,* and modernized the *Louvre* at Paris which was a Medieval fortress. In the Gothic interior the fireplace had been the main feature of the irregularly shaped room. In this transitional period the fireplace was still monumental and hooded, similar to Gothic examples, except that it boasted small classic pilasters and cornices. The ceilings were enriched by structural beams and girders painted in a profusion of stripes and ornaments. The floors were often laid with tiles in beautiful highly colored patterns. Walls were paneled in the Gothic style with wood, often ornamented with delicate arabesques, or covered with decorated Cordova leather. The furniture was the heavy rectangular type, but decorated with classic architectural motifs.

As the great halls of the Middle Ages gave place to smaller living rooms, lighting fixtures lost their monumental character. Beauty of outline and proportion was enriched by finely worked ornament in typical Renaissance designs. France made fuller use of floral and conventional forms than of the mythological and whimsical motifs popular in Italy. With the increasing amenities of domestic life and social functions, demand for a more even lighting of the smaller rooms then in fashion resulted in the perfecting of certain types of fixtures like the wall bracket, the hanging chandelier, and the candelabra. *Torchères, bougeoirs* with *mouchettes*—snuffers, and other candlesticks were beautified with Renaissance ornament. The name *bougeoir* seems to have fallen into disuse in the 16th Century. Snuffers were attached to the small hand candlesticks in common use. A *chandelier palmatoir*—hand candlestick, recalls Spain's *palmatoria;* while the elaborately encrusted ornamentation on a long-stemmed candlestick was known as work in the *mode d'Espaigne,* reminiscent of the splendor of Spanish Renaissance silverware. A lovely candle-holder of *argent doré* and red enamel to fasten to the headboard of a bed was made in the same style.

The typical candlestick and candelabrum of the period had the Renaissance outline of foot, stem, and socket—*pied, tige,* and *cuvette;* usually turned, and of bronze with two or three *nœuds*—knops.

More elaborate examples were often correspondingly whimsical. A pair of bronze candlesticks (Fig. 34) though of Renaissance inspiration, have a peculiar mixture of both form and ornament, suggesting Romanesque, Gothic, and Renaissance influences.

Turn the illustration upside down and it will be clear that the designer had made use of the well-known form of the *tassa*—short-stemmed cup, with a gadrooned cover and a knob which when inverted is held just off the table by four scrolled feet. Complete mastery of Renaissance design is evident in the formation of these

34. A pair of 16th Century *chandeliers* in bronze elaborated with Renaissance motifs and figures but suggestive of earlier ornament. Courtesy French & Co.

feet. Each consists of a woman's bust, reclining against the cup, the shoulders ending in vigorous scrolling in place of arms, the body terminating in the Renaissance manner in acanthus leaf scrolls which continue to form the foot, but with the evident swirling of the mermaid form. Upon the broad plateau formed by the bottom of the cup's foot, four crouching figures struggle to uphold four tall composite ornaments bedecking the sides of the ovoid vase which rests on the plateau. These ornaments rise vertically like a totem pole, one motif above the other, terminating in four women's busts, a crown topping each head. The motifs between are formed of leaf scrolls like the Renaissance foliated dolphin heads, but with extra grimacing reminiscent of the open-mouthed classic masks of the actor, the Chinese *tao-teh* ogre, and the dragons of Romanesque and Gothic days. The vase form of the stem supports an excellent classic urn to hold the candle, but its body is exaggerated with four medallions in high relief each centered with a woman's mask. The vigor of this design is astonishing. Its squirm suggests the English Gloucester Candlestick of the 12th Century (Fig. 69) and French work of the Gothic and Romanesque periods, while its decorative motifs are clearly those of the Renaissance. It is a fine example of that energetic emphasis of local variant which developed the distinctly native style of Louis XIV.

Prickets were still in use in the *chandelier à verges*—with rod or stem. The *chandelier à la romaine* in vogue at the end of the 16th Century was designed like a Roman column with base and capital. It was made in silver, bronze, and copper. All the metals were requisitioned: silver and silver-gilt adorned with ivory and semi-precious stones, bronze, copper, brass, and pewter; and the fixtures were rarely beautiful.

Flanders influenced French silverware in *le style Hollandaise*. Silver in turn influenced pewter. One pair of 16th Century candlesticks in *étain*—pewter, made by François Birot are as superb as if cast in silver. The nozzle is a wide-mouthed urn beautifully shaped, and the upper part of the stem is formed like an inverted cup from which the lower stem recedes gracefully to a narrow base above the plateau. The stem is round and decorated with *mascarons*—masks, and garlands. A sphinx with a woman's body is surrounded by palmettes and foliage—*de rinceau*. The stem rests upon a large circular plateau decorated with four oval medallions, allegorical figures, and figures representing the seasons. The three feet are formed of women's busts.

Wood was carved, silvered, gilded, and polychromed especially in red, green, and blue. Some of the oldest known wooden candlesticks date from the Renaissance. They were usually for the large Paschal candles. Both large and small candlesticks were made of precious metals, heavy ones for the French kings and for the

Church. Altar candlesticks increased in height, from the 16th to the 18th Centuries. Superb candlesticks of glazed and colored pottery with elaborate Renaissance ornament were made of *Oiron* ware, known also as *Henri Deux* ware. This was a most extraordinary type of pottery made near Oiron from 1530–60, much of it during the reign of *Henri Deux* (1549–59) and now named for him. It is made of a fine white clay covered with a lead glaze. The designs are in high relief and include typical Renaissance motifs such as human figures, wreaths, escutcheons, shells, etc. Their peculiar interest to the lover of ceramics is that some of these designs are impressed into the body of the piece with different colored clays. The work is highly decorative and a *Henri Deux* candlestick is truly an *objet d'art*. Such candlesticks preserve pure Renaissance outlines and are comparable to the metal-work of the period.

There are only about eighty pieces of this ware known. They show great variety in form and ornament without duplication. The Victoria and Albert Museum has a candlestick of *Oiron* ware made in the typical Renaissance form and beautifully decorated. The name of a woman, Hélène de Hanest-Genlis, is closely associated with this pottery. She was either a patron of the work or may possibly have worked at the pottery. The pieces are elaborately enriched with bold relief ornament, engraving, and decoration of arabesques, interlacings, and initial letters formed of different colored clays impressed into the hollowed design producing a smoothly decorated surface like fine inlay or damascening. It is covered with a thin yellowish transparent glaze.

In the early 16th Century some Italian potters came to Lyons and established a new type of pottery. *Henri Deux* himself was in Lyons in 1548. Italian maiolica was in its decline at the time and many potters and painters of this ware emigrated to France. The candlesticks were not as common as other pieces but they were available in French *faience* in the modes of the period.

Wall brackets—*appliques* or *bras de lumière* were always of peculiar interest to the French designer and seem to have been much appreciated even in the earlier periods. With the Renais-

sance came a great enriching of this fixture with new designs and
ornament. Iron was not abandoned and Gothic forms were only
gradually superseded. One made in the early Renaissance in the
style of Henry II (Fig. 35) shows Italian influence in the upper
curve of the large supporting C-scroll which in terminating di-
vides and turns back over the body of the scroll which it straddles.
Spanish influence is evident in the naturalistic tassels of iron
bedecking the lambrequin edging the bottom of the corona. The

35. This Henri II *applique* of wrought-iron shows Spanish influence in its iron
tassels and Italian in its straddled turned-back scrolling. Courtesy Bagués, Inc.

foliage ornamenting the bracket enriches it in the Renaissance
manner. It is highly sophisticated for a piece of ironwork.

Hanging lights were not yet known by the familiar French name
of *lustre* but they were beautifully made in Renaissance branch
work of wood, bronze, and silver. Francis I ordered one in silver
in 1538 of Guilliaume Herondelle, a Parisian silversmith. Carved
and gilded wooden chandeliers with four or five branches highly
ornate with leafage and Renaissance scrolling, masks, and vase
forms were used in the queen's chambers and in fine houses. They
were in special favor for dining-rooms from the 16th to the 18th
Century. The *applique* or *bras de lumière* was designed in the
same manner. Copper and bronze were elaborately worked in two-

tiered chandeliers, and by the end of the 16th Century metal chandeliers especially of bronze were in current use. They were profusely decorated with figures, birds, etc.; and shells often formed the *bobèches*. Chandeliers of animal horns and iron from Germany were still in fashion as in Gothic days, but coronas were little seen except for temporary festival illumination. Bronze was the Renaissance metal as iron had been the Gothic. *Dinanderie* appeared occasionally, for we find those whimsical pieces noted as *"ces belles pièces de dinanderie."* Rock-crystal was employed to some degree to ornament hanging lights, forerunners of the marvelous crystal chandeliers of the Louis XIV period.

Kitchen lamps persisted in the ancient ancestral form of the *candile,* both open and covered. But the lamp was to receive considerable attention in France where many inventions added to its effectiveness for practical use. Cardan invented a lamp that could be raised and lowered and which regulated the flow of oil, a factor closely considered in the following periods. Oil lamps were still mounted on candlesticks—*chandeliers à huile,* and had the oil regulated in a primitive way during the reign of Henry III (1574–89). By an ingenious contrivance a lamp was made in the early 16th century which indicated the passing of time like a clock. Fragrant oils were burned by the rich. Olive oil was in more common use as in Italy and Spain.

Lanterns received great attention and were splendidly designed for decorative effect, either architecturally or in the well-known rectangular Renaissance model which slopes a little toward the bottom. Their workmanship was as fine as their designs which were frequently resplendent with elaborate motifs of the period.

In the reign of *Henri II* (1547–1610), Gothic forms were more completely eliminated, and a fuller use was made of their local variants; for the style of *François I* (1515–47) had been that of a Gothic body with Italian Renaissance clothing. The Italian spirit, alive with the beauty and grandeur of Greece and Rome, finally prevailed. Slavish imitation was not to be thought of with such sprightly people as the French and local influences gradually developed a truly native style. Few definite steps in the progress of any of the arts is noticeable however in the years between 1547 and 1610 which was a period of study and development for the French artist.

Fireplaces were still prominent in the interior and the hearth light still a factor in winter illumination. Color enriched the ceilings which were beamed, paneled, coffered, or plastered, and further embellished with inlay and gilding. Floors were of marble tiling or parqueted wood. Walls were paneled in various shapes with larger panels than formerly, often carved, gilded, and inlaid. Entire walls were frescoed, or frescoed panels were framed in plaster moldings. The furniture included the same articles used in Italy in the Renaissance, arranged around the walls except for occasional convenience. Candlesticks and candelabra with highly elaborated ornament in classic forms were the most conspicuous furnishing accessory.

With the assimilation of the art impulse from Renaissance Italy, France's native art instinct was most vigorously aroused in the period usually classed as the Baroque. Supported by royal patronage and royal institutions it grew to a conscious mastery of art forms and art materials. The Baroque style in France dates from the reign of Louis XIII (1610–43), who succeeded his father Henry IV, with his mother Marie de Medici as regent. Richelieu, who wore alternately the cardinal's hat and the helmet of a generalissimo in the French army, made Louis XIII "the first man in Europe, but the second in his kingdom." Richelieu virtually ruled France. He crushed the Protestant Huguenots, and in so doing the art crafts of the world were blessed; for these Huguenots were skillful craftsmen and took their skill with them, especially to the Netherlands and England. But Richelieu was nevertheless a great patron of art and letters and has to his credit the establishment of the French Academy. He brought magnificence to a point of great expectation, so that it remained for artists in France under the patronage of Louis XIV to crystallize the first of the distinctly national French styles—*le style Louis Quatorze*. This is the great period of French lighting fixtures, as the Renaissance was in Italy, and the Gothic in Spain. Hanging and wall-lights took on enormous importance and even the candlestick became a distinguished decorative accessory.

The opening of the 17th Century was the period of the lamp, for the 16th Century had perfected the use of the wax candle. Much study was given the mechanical phase of the lamp, upon which the art form more or less depended. It is claimed that Cardan's earlier invention was not actually applied until the 17th Century. Lamps were not in such general use as in the 18th Century but a number of forms were developed, all quite simple however; usually set up on a short stem, or a mere oil cup with fixed or movable handles as in the *lampes suspendus* for hanging. They were made of copper, pewter, pottery, etc.

While economic ideas went into the making of lamps, art still spent itself in the making of candle-holders, from the splendid crystal chandeliers of Louis XIV's palace at *Versailles* to the *appliques* of *bronze doré* or *ormolu*, perhaps with crystal pendants, the *girandoles, lanternes,* and above all the baluster candlesticks which then held sway as they do to this day among ourselves. The little *bougeoir* was a necessity, from the humble one of iron and that of *bronze argenté*—silvered, to the superb *bougeoir* held at the bedside of the king, a ceremony of rigid observance under the strict rules of etiquette which were formulated at the Court of *Louis Quatorze.*

Candlesticks were now called *flambeaux* instead of *chandeliers.* There were *flambeaux de salle, de table,* and *de chambre,* made in precious metal or silvered bronze. Three hundred and twenty-four of the *flambeaux* at Versailles were of silver, *argent blanc*—white silver, that is, not gilt. Most of them were made in baluster form. The stems of the older ones were round, square, or polygonal. But the silverware of Louis XIV with that of all France went into the melting pot of war in 1689 so that little remains. Designs for candlesticks, *torchères, girandoles,* etc., by Bérain, Germain, Ballin, Marot, Blondel, and Stella have left us models seldom equaled and rarely surpassed. Foliage and figures were supremely handled: nudes, loves, satyrs, masks, etc.; the acanthus scrolling was magnificent. Louis XIII fixtures showed the mingling of Flemish and

Italian ornament characteristic of the period; many of them were
massive and classic. Louis XIV types employed trophies of victory, horns of plenty, and arms, with insistence on the *amours*—
little cupids, which the king loved. The *chandelier à la financière*
had a slide to raise and lower the candle, a common contrivance
since that day. *Candélabres* and *girandoles* were elaborated, both
with two or more branches, the *girandole* for wall, table, or elaborate flat-topped pedestal called *torchère;* the *girandole* was usually
more simple than the *candélabre,* the only distinction which seems
to have been made in the use of the term.

Chandeliers d'applique received the same minute attention from
the greatest designers as did the other fixtures. Prior to the reign
of Louis XIII, these wall brackets were largely utilitarian. Now
the backplates were highly elaborated and beautifully made of
wrought-iron, bronze, or other metals, and wood. A typical example of an *applique* or *bras* of the early Louis XIII period (Fig.
36) is in the form of a vigorous human arm securely holding a
short fluted column spreading widely into a conventionalized
petaled flower which supports a large urn socket with a flaring
bowl-shaped mouth suggestive of the grease pans of older candlesticks. The arm and hand are well modeled, the standard excellent,
and the wall-plate of scrolled ribbons in a thick rounded twist,
with a rolled-up sleeve on the arm, shows the good workmanship
of the entire piece. It is made of oak and polychromed; the hand
and arm flesh colored, the wall piece blue, red, and gilt.

Another wall bracket of the Louis XIII period has a walnut
backplate boldly carved in an escutcheon, and gilded. A simple
flat horizontal bar is secured in the center of the shield and upholds a three-branched iron bracket. The center upright terminates
in a scalloped arrow-like finial below a vandyked disk. Above this
on a vertical plane, two branches spring outward horizontally, are
bent in an easy rounded corner and ascend upward, making three
parallel uprights, the middle one slightly the taller. These were
to hold the very long candles of the day. There are no grease
pans, but the stems terminate in a pricket with four sharp-pointed
upturning leaves like a flower calix. Two pairs of simple C-shaped

scrolls ornament the uprights at intervals, with a formalized flower-like motif springing outward from the bend of the outer branches. A short flat cross-bar just above their juncture makes the sign of the cross.

Mirror backs—*plaques en miroir,* were precious things. Many *appliques* were simple (Fig. VI), some highly ornate with candle branches held by figures especially of women and children, terminating in acanthus scrolling. Other typical Louis XIV motifs

36. Carved oak Renaissance *bras,* polychromed. Early Louis XIII. Italian influence. Courtesy Bagués, Inc.

such as satyrs, heads, masks, etc., were frequently used. Some *appliques* had movable branches.

The hanging lights, called *candélabres* in the 17th Century, were sumptuous. They are known as *lustres* to-day, the name given them in the 18th Century. The Louis XIII preference was for those chandeliers of brass from the Netherlands which gained such a vogue in Europe that they were as much at home in English rooms as in French. They were of enormous weight for the central shaft was solid. It was designed in baluster form composed of vase motifs or a series of large balls connected by turned members. Another type of chandelier retained the hexagonal coronas, usually two, joined with S-shaped scrolling in the earlier modes but delicately designed and very attractive in its incorporation of well

VI. This handsome Louis XIV *applique* of brass incorporates an oval convex metal plaque in the wall-plate to increase the candle-light, and shows an early use of the ribbon bow-knot. Courtesy Bagués, Inc.

shaped vase motifs. Wooden chandeliers were often extremely beautiful but they were rarer than the metal ones. They were in use until the mid-17th Century. Both were made in small and large sizes. French artists like Bérain and Boulle made wonderful designs for chandeliers: flying cupids bore the candles; canopies and swags adorned them; huge globes were surmounted by

37. This superb Louis XIV *bronze doré candélabre*—chandelier, is typical of the finest work of the period. Courtesy French· & Co.

women's figures; splendid scrolled branches swung outward, ornate with acanthus leaves (Fig. 37) especially in the Louis XIV period; and they were topped by great crowns. These fixtures were usually of *bronze doré* though a few were as elaborately conceived in iron and some in silver.

The crystal *lustre* was inspired by Italy. The superb examples

in the *galerie des glaces* at *Versailles* are well known. The variety
in cutting the pendants on a single piece is astonishing, and prized
by the modern antiquarian happy enough to possess one of these
rare early pieces. By 1657 crystal chandeliers were found in many
homes. The most distinctive feature of these crystal-hung chan-

38. Variety of outline gives charm to the pendants of this magnificent Louis
XIV brass and crystal chandelier. Courtesy French & Co.

deliers of the Louis XIV period is the shaping of their metal
framework. Usually of brass, the metal supports took on a vase or
jar form, tending toward the lyre-shape at the end of this period.
These frames were more or less closely hung (Fig. 38) with hand-
cut pendants of the costly semiprecious rock-crystal, later imitated
in crystal and the less costly glass. Their tops still kept the
bouquet motif which had crowned so many fixtures since Gothic
days. Occasionally a small garland appeared, but the usual method
was to hang each pendant from a crystal star or marguerite. A

large ball was the usual finial, while occasionally small bouquets or slender faceted pyramids or spires were placed around the middle of the piece, breaking the monotony of the pendants.

This was the age of the silk cord and tassel which the Moors brought so lavishly to Spain, and we are not surprised to find these chandeliers hung magnificently. This type of garnishment is called a *cartisane* or cord, the tassel itself is a *gland*, and the elaborated silk canopy that holds the cord against the ceiling—a *pavillon*.

A word about *cuivre doré, ormolu,* and *bronze doré. Cuivre doré* is copper gilded with gold leaf, a costly product. *Bronze doré* is treated in the same manner. *Ormolu* was made by the process of mercury gilding. The mercury process was difficult and seemingly hazardous, so that new processes are used to-day but they never surpass and hardly equal the beauty of this older work. The use of these gilded metals was particularly appropriate for lighting fixtures in rooms where metal mounts of the same materials had so conspicuous a place on the furniture. Boulle, the famous cabinet-maker, popularized *ormolu* and brass ornaments, which in this and the succeeding periods were works of art. Ceremonious rooms at this time were of enormous size with massive architectural and furniture detail. Wall paneling was large, vigorous, and rectangular, placed above a dado. It was often of natural oak; frequently cream colored with gilt moldings; and occasionally in other colorings. Wood carving was elaborate; fireplaces conspicuous; paintings were framed in the overmantels, as were mirrors; doors were paneled, carved, painted, and gilded; the floors were of parquet, marble, or tiling.

Lanterns were magnificent. There were several types in typical period designs. The Renaissance rectangular model was the favorite. French designers showed their usual discrimination in the making of these lanterns. The faint light within served rather to illuminate their beauty than aught else. Some Renaissance types were fitted with candle branches outside the body of the lantern to augment the light. From the time of Louis XIII carved and gilded wood was used superbly in large decorative lanterns.

Architectural types prevailed whether of iron or more precious metals. The framework was resplendent with ornament in the elaborate style of the period. Louis XIII examples showed a blending of Flemish and Italian influences, while Louis XIV examples were distinctly French and usually of bronze or wood. The *demi-*

39. Carved, gilded, and polychromed linden wood in a splendid design. *Lanterne* of the late Louis XIII and early Louis XIV period. Scrolled bottom and crown distinctly Louis XIII; cornice Louis XIV. Courtesy Bagués, Inc.

lanterne—a half lantern, which fitted against the wall was a contrivance of the Louis XIV period and was ornamented in the style of the day. A superb linden wood lantern (Fig. 39) made at the end of the reign of Louis XIII or at the beginning of that of Louis XIV, combines elements current in both reigns. The tin crown is Louis XIII, so is the bottom of the lantern, but the cornice bespeaks the work favored by Louis XIV when the architectural orders were employed in the wood and plaster moldings and ornaments of a room, as in the door and window framing and the overmantel. Glittering gold and crystal were always in evidence, skillfully calculated to symbolize the reign of *Louis Quatorze* who delighted in the title of *"le roi soleil."*

CHAPTER V

LOUIS XV

THE 18th Century was supreme on both sides of the Atlantic for comfort combined with beauty in the homes of the English speaking race. How much of that beauty and comfort was inspired by French taste and ingenuity becomes evident when we inspect the interiors and furnishings that France has had the discernment and ability to preserve for her own good and the good of the world. This conservation, in spite of the ravages of wars, has kept intact much to delight all who are interested in what constitutes good interiors.

Of all the period styles, that of *Louis Quinze* (1715–1774) has perhaps the greatest fascination for those deeply learned in interior decoration, while the very word *Rococo,* with which it has been labeled, often provokes contempt from those who take their taste in art second-hand. The style was not actually confined to the years during the reign of Louis XV. The insatiable human craving for variety and change swings the pendulum forward and back from the extreme of formality, stateliness, and pomp, which in time grow stereotyped, to that individual expression which tends to break bounds and become whimsical and extravagant. The dominance of Louis XIV's great minister, Colbert, perfected such organized artistic activities as western Europe had never seen. But it was under this very dominance that the chafing at restraint actually showed itself in the beginnings of *le style Louis Quinze,* growing more pronounced during the *Régence* (1715–1723)—the Regency of Louis XV's childhood, and coming to florescence in the supreme achievements of the Rococo style during his reign.

This was the period when the French people, after their splendid tutelage under Colbert, developed that indescribable quality of choice we call "good taste," for which they are still world-famous. This taste was built along no single line of achievement, but had the inspiration of the most gifted and skillful artists and designers working in every material and with every object, from the walls, ceilings, lighting fixtures, furniture, and textiles, to the panel of my lady's sedan chair, her exquisite little fan, and the very lace that beruffled her dress. Just as a French costume is perfected by minute attention to each detail, not one point neglected, so a French period interior is achieved. The lighting fixtures become organic elements in the ensemble and can be comprehended only when so considered. This does not mean that *Louis Quinze* lighting fixtures cannot be used in any room but one in strict period style. They can be introduced, just as other French accessories and furniture are discriminatingly introduced, so that they add that element of gayety, that *élan,* that delicate, occasionally humorous touch inseparably connected with this period of social life in France, when a Du Barry might use a little pickaninny for her footstool, and woman ruled King and Court by the tap of her tiny fan.

While much thought was being given at this time to the economic use of oil in lamps, the lamp itself never inspired the artist as it did in the days of ancient Rome. Vase forms were used for hanging lamps, and candlestick shapes for table lamps, but these were often ugly and made of varnished and decorated tin. Simple ancient types like the *veilleuse*—night lamp, were occasionally bejeweled and of gold, making a luxurious ornament for the mantel. The accepted lighting of the period however was still candle-light; therefore exquisite workmanship and joyful designing were lavished on candle fixtures.

The kinds of fixtures were much the same as in the reign of Louis XIV: hand candlesticks, table candlesticks, ceremonious table and occasionally floor candelabra, chandeliers, wall-lights, lanterns, and the practical and homely lamp. But there were variations of these fixtures, and a delightful, even affectionate, adaptation of them to the social habits of the times. One such adaptation was the use of candle brackets attached to various articles of furniture, particularly writing desks and mirrors. Supported on pedestals and wall brackets, the *girandoles* appear as an integral part of the design of these decorative accessories. Charming little tables—candle stands, were in vogue, and these trifles became indispensable to every well conducted household just as they did in England and America.

The *bougeoir,* that one might carry about the room, or from room to room, was ordinarily quite simple, of tin, iron, brass, pewter, plain bronze, *bronze doré* and *argenté,* silver, or gold. It had a flat saucer-like base, a socket or nozzle set directly on this base, and a convenient handle. But this object of convenience was also made to conform to its surroundings, and workmanship no less artistic than that expended on the finest jewelry went into its making. Some *bougeoirs* were exquisite fantasies, capriciously set with brilliants and were much more ornamental than practical. The *bougeoir de lit*—bed candlestick, was a mechanical contrivance of *cuivre doré* or *ormolu,* usually with an oval *plateau—* plate, a shade—*garde-vue,* and an extinguisher—*éteignoir.*

The taller candlestick, now known as *flambeau,* also received minute attention. Baluster stems, those symmetrical shapes we connect with old stair balusters, took on infinite variety in the *Louis Quatorze* period only to be neglected for shapes known as dissymmetrical, where the outline of one side is not actually repeated, as in a vase or urn, but each side is varied as in a whimsically shaped leaf. This type of outline accorded with the decorative ornament known as *rocaille* or *rococo*—a handful of swirling curves and crimps twisted this way and that with the whim of nature in forming the rocks and shells, *rocaille* signifying a mingling of water-worn rockery and shell forms. But through all this inorganic and fantastic scrolling emerged the more natural leaf forms of the acanthus, which few artists can abandon when once their pencils begin to dally with its fascinating possibility of scroll and swirl and curve. Because of our interest in this subject of the acanthus, beloved of designers since the days of Greece, we actually grew an acanthus plant and so fell completely under its spell ourselves.

The reign of Louis XV was the era of *bronze doré* and crystal. We find the most beautiful conceptions of the period worked out in these materials and sold by jewelers as precious things. Silver and gold were, of course, used by royalty and the very rich, but artists of the period made some of their most delightful designs in *cuivre* or *bronze argenté* or *doré,* and in crystal. Steel, ornamented with *bronze doré,* was also popular.

True *cuivre argenté* is pure copper, cast—that is, *cuivre fondu,* or hand wrought—*cuivre battu,* and covered with silver-leaf or liquid. Mixed with tin, copper becomes *bronze* and is cast and gilded, or silvered. Tin is *tôle* and brass is *laiton.* We do not use the terms accurately to-day, and *cuivre doré* may mean any gilded

40. Dissymmetrical form in this *bronze doré flambeau* is typical of *le style Louis Quinze.* Courtesy Bagués, Inc.

metal. Copper silvered keeps its silver white; while with bronze, the tin in the bronze which gives its ring to bell metal, eats into the silver and blackens it. *Bronze ciselé*—chiseled, gave the needed touch to sharpen the lines in Rococo ornament, and brought out the fine detail characteristic of the style.

A bronze candlestick of the period (Fig. 40) with sharply defined ornament may be so slightly dissymmetrical as to appear little divergent from the baluster form of earlier days. Still the swirl at the base of the somewhat emphasized candle socket, and the leaf ornaments trailed over the base class it as Louis XV.

Porcelain candlesticks were made in the Chinese style. The mantel and console table garnitures of the 18th Century doubtless had their inspiration in vases, covered urns, and candlesticks imported from China at this time. Their origin goes back thousands of years to the time when bronzes in similar shapes formed the garniture for the altar in ancient Chinese worship. This idea of arranging ornamental vases, urns, or clock, and candlesticks to compose a garniture is characteristic of the 18th Century interior. The vogue for *cuivre doré* or *ormolu* mountings was carried to such an extent that costly Chinese porcelain vases were elaborately mounted with metal bases and covers and often encased more or less completely in decorative metal swags and scrolls. Fine furniture was often almost covered in the same way, abandoning woodcarving for the resplendence of metallic mounts. On the corners of writing desks these mounts often terminated in candle branches of practical lighting aid. The designs were either Rococo branch work and leafage, or were figures of women or cupids upholding branch work or simple candle cups.

Table candlesticks with stems, and *candélabres* with several branches for candles were not the only forms. The *surtout de table*, for the center of the dining-table, charmingly elaborated, became a decorative necessity in every important household. Of silver if possible, merely silvered if not. The typical design was based on some version of a large jar or vase incorporated in an elaborate curvilinear structure set up on feet and supporting scrolled candle branches. Designs such as those by Meissonier included human figures, satyrs, nymphs, etc. The scrolled candle branches were often an integral part of the ornament and not superimposed, and the feet variously shaped, often merely a scrolled leaf.

The *chandelier brule-bouts*, a candlestick with a mechanical contrivance to keep the candle flame at a certain height and still burn the very last of the candle, was invented by Duchateau.

Girandoles in *cuivre argenté* were used on dining-tables where candlesticks and the usual small hanging *lustres* were insufficient. To these might be added a pair of low candlesticks from three to eight inches in height holding one or two candles. Because they were placed at the end of the table such candlesticks were called *bout de table* or table-end candlesticks. *Girandoles* were beautifully designed with fantasies as delectable as the greatest artists of the day could conceive: satyrs' heads peered through ivy festoons; cymbals, Pan's pipes, cupids, and scrolled acanthus leafage adorned them. It must be remembered that the *girandole,* as the French use the word, referred to the branched light, whether a wall-light or detached like a candelabrum. It was often placed on the *torchère* of that day, a highly ornate carved and gilded pedestal with a flat top, or on top of a small carved wall bracket designed for the purpose. When placed on a bracket, pedestal, mantel, or against the wall, the design was so adapted as to throw the candle branches forward into a semicircle, though often an irregular one.

One of this type (Fig. 41) made of bronze hung with crystal is based on a triangular scroll-edged plateau which supports the scrolled tripod feet, and from their juncture spring the lyre-shaped supports. These terminate in drooping scrolls from which depend large flat pendants topped by marguerites. In the center of this spray-like bouquet—again reminiscent of early iron *candélabre* designs, rises a tall elaborately faceted spire or pyramid. The candle branches spring from the tripod in swelling upward curves in line with the lower curving of the lyre supports. From these branches and the supports, large flat pendants are hung, each topped by its daisy flower. The conception is exquisite. *Girandoles* usually carried the candle sockets dissymmetrically on different levels and reversed in pairs. Figures might hold branch lights. The typical model was a child's figure mounted on a short column and bearing a branch of flowers in which were candle sockets. Cabinet pieces were made of groups of porcelain figures, especially those from Saxony, sometimes mounted in *ormolu.* Monumental candelabra, like the floor lights of earlier days, were rare.

The *applique* of the period was particularly charming. The *bras de cheminée* on either side of the mirror over a fireplace was as interesting as the *garniture de cheminée* which decked the mantel, incorporating porcelains and brilliants and other extraneous materials in many capricious designs.

Styles in lighting fixtures were all of a piece with the other furnishings, and they underwent the same transformation. The ornamentation of the fixture was the fixture (Fig. 42). The fixture was not a frame with ornament. The ornament was the fixture.

41. *Girandole* of bronze and crystal with typical lyre-shaped supports, daisies and flat leaf-shaped pendants. Courtesy Bagués, Inc.

Examine any *applique* and this fact becomes evident. A typical three-branched one of *bronze doré* (Fig. 43), a superb example, is composed wholly of swirling branches suggestive of growing stems or stalks of irregular outline bedecked with long leaves clasping these stems and curving off into the rounded point of the oak leaf. Naturally formed oak leaves and acorns spread along the branch work and spring out naturally from it where it breaks into a sharp bend. They also form a circle below each candle socket, like a grease pan, and overlapping they form the socket as well. Rustic work with graded piercing and a complete circling scroll lighten and balance the design. But not an inch of the framework is a mere frame; the frame itself is built up of ornament.

Another example (Fig. 44), and both of these *appliques* are

42. This *ormolu applique* in dissymmetrical Rococo form has a saucy bat-winged grotesque with tail entwining the bottom of the fixture. Courtesy French & Co.

made in pairs with reversed design to flank the chimneypiece or other paneling, is of *ormolu*. The handling of the metal is as different from that of the three-branched *bronze doré applique* as one person's handwriting is from another's. There is a suavity and fluency to this *ormolu applique* that seems almost incredible, more like the actual growing leaf than mere metal. The long narrow leaf that outlines the circle in which the griffin nests is especially so conceived. Here as in the *bronze doré applique* no frame crops out at any point; leaf emerges from leaf, under and over with that spring of the growing stalk that is marvelous. The socket and *bobèche* both swirl in petaled floral forms. Leaf clusters finish the piece in a pendant group and top the griffin's nest. This wily beast-bird creeps undaunted from its swirling lair like so many of the whimsical grotesques of the period.

Wood was no less expertly handled in these *appliques* but does not always proclaim itself for what it is at a glance. It is scarcely

43. An exquisite example of Rococo scrolling enlivened by natural oak leaves and acorns, in a three-branched *applique* of *bronze doré*. Courtesy Bagués, Inc.

less sprightly than the metal but a trifle heavier looking. There are the same swirls of growing things terminating in leaf ends; but flowers cluster here and there with their sprigs of leafage, and the wood suggests a tree trunk and its accompanying growth. There is no open piercing or circling swirl, the detail of natural growth is more closely followed. The sockets and grease pans offer the same swirling outlines, but more deeply scalloped for the *bobèche* and more formalized for the socket; gilding enlivens the whole.

Other examples in wood sometimes spread their side branches more broadly in as great a variety of dissymmetry as nature herself, whom the artist keeps closely in mind.

Working in designs more frankly floral (Fig. 45), like the colored metal-work typical of Rouen, the quality of the growing stem is more naturalistically conceived and the flower sprays are more detached. The leaves too take on more natural forms, however conventionalized and fanciful the flowers, but the *bobèche* and socket abandon the Rococo at times and become what they really are, a flat saucer and a tall cup-shaped socket, both painted with a conventional design. The bracket and flowers are brightly colored on a mellow cream ground. Although there were some distinctive models of fixtures, like the *surtout,* developed in the *Louis Quinze* style, the ornamenting of the fixtures was the important thing.

44. One of a pair of *ormolu appliques.* To the purely conventionalized Rococo scrolling is added naturalistic leaf forms and a griffin in her lair. Courtesy French & Co.

This became attenuated, delicate, less any one single thing except the sprightly swirling of Rococo curves, giving the silhouette typical of the period which imposed itself upon candlestick, candelabrum, bracket, and chandelier.

The transition from the classical character of *Louis Quatorze* fixtures to the Rococo of *Louis Quinze* in *le style Régence* has many admirers. Freed from restraint and not yet effeminate, it is vigorous yet individual; neither so dainty nor so formal; but regal and handsome. *Régence* designs may be recognized by their mingling of well defined formal curved outlines and swirls, reminiscent of the Baroque character of *Louis Quatorze,* with

Rococo leaf ornament; while *Louis Quinze* designs worked out the entire branch work in irregular Rococo swirls or leaf forms, amid which cupids, grotesques, or other figures playfully regarded each other and trunks of trees and rustic scrollwork stems terminated in flower cups for candle nozzles. At *Versailles* some of the State apartments were cut up into small *salons*. The with-drawing room, which in England and America developed into the drawing-room, had its inception at this time. There was a tendency to use

45. A typical example of work from Rouen in an enameled metal *applique* with flowers and leaves brightly colored on a mellow cream ground. Courtesy French & Co.

the rooms of a house, even a palace, for every-day living, instead of reserving them for parade and display. Elegance superseded grandeur. Everything was scaled down. Mantelpieces were small and useful, charmingly designed with those swinging free-hand scrolls not an inch of which can be accomplished by mechanical compass. To those who study this type of ornament appreciatively this scrollwork holds as individual an interest as does the chirography for the oriental. It is as individual and unmistakable as one's handwriting, with a certain recognizable swing to it. The French Rococo was the consummation of elegance and finesse when carried out by the best artists of the period in the spirit of the day. It sometimes became exaggerated and often tawdry when appropriated by Italy and Spain, and—must we say it?—by England.

With the wall-lights of the *Régence* and *Louis Quinze* periods, the room itself must be considered, so integral a part of the interior decoration did the wall-lights become. The typical *Régence* room with its low dado, its chimney piece reaching the coved ceiling, and its walls paneled in tapestry, incorporated its wall-lights—*appliques* or *girandoles,* as part of its design. Nicholas Pineau, artist and wood carver, made vigorous designs for *girandoles* which hint of Italy with their *mascarons* and outstanding carving; some have a scrolled backplate lined by a mirror, over the face of which are splendid festoons. His brackets, highly fantastic with scroll and leafwork, griffins, lions, and cupids, have a flat top to accommodate a candelabrum. His branched lights to be placed at either side of a mirror are beautifully attenuated in irregular scrolling with inconspicuous candle sockets. *Bras de lumière* for furniture or mirrors had extraordinary leaf and floral forms, with urn-shaped sockets set in a corona of leaves, the stems following the reversed curves in leaf and scroll so typical of the later Rococo style. Mirrors were much used as backplates for wall-lights and followed the statelier mode of *Louis Quatorze* models in their elaborately shaped frames, but in a sprightlier spirit. Cupids often held the candle branches. Scrolled metal-work without glass also formed the backplates for such wall-lights.

A splendid example of a *Régence applique* (Fig. 46), with a mirror wall-plate and frame of carved and gilded wood, has all the dashing magnificence of the *Louis Quatorze* style, with a suavity and individuality peculiar to the *Régence*. The mirror is finished with a curved molding shaped to spread at the top and with cut corners, just the proper beginning for the highly ornamental cresting above. This is accomplished with a crown of leafage set up on a well formed pediment, the abrupt lines of which offer the typical contrast to the Rococo curves which marks the style *Régence*. The two lower crests at the cut corners have typical Rococo foliations but include an abruptly defined C-scroll over which is draped a weary griffin. The mirror frame follows the outline of the mirror to the lower ornamentation, which includes floral and leaf bouquets and three splendidly carved C-scrolled candle branches in *Régence* design with magnificently foliated *bobèches* which also act as candle sockets.

Another *Régence* example (Fig. 47), with a much larger mirror on which the candle branches are merely accessory, shows even

46. A highly decorative *applique* of carved and gilded wood; the wall-plate set with a mirror. Formal scrolls distinctly outlined amid the Rococo leafage distinguish it as a *Régence* piece. Courtesy Bagués, Inc.

more distinctly the transition between the Baroque and Rococo almost to the point of the conglomerate, the two styles mixed but not mingled. The voluptuous carved scrollwork is draped and interspersed with naturalistic ornaments of various kinds. The cresting is a formalized almost shell-like interpretation of the well-known five-feather motif. Within their curved tips is a basket-like crown surrounding a vase filled with roses and their foliage naturally and beautifully carved. From the upstanding corner scrolls decked with naturalistic leaves, depend swags which support groups of naturally formed shells. Below the corner scrolls are well filled horns of plenty, and below these flanking the long rectangular mirror are rustic oak branches with acorns carved in the most natural manner. Other types of leafage spring from the juncture of the pair of candle brackets on each side of the mirror. These brackets are also a mixture of styles, the frankly visible frame being ornamented with oak leaves and acorns. The bottom

47. Baroque and Rococo elements are combined but not assimilated in the framing of this *Régence* mirror with its *cuivre doré* candle brackets. Courtesy The Anderson Galleries.

of the mirror is decorated with formal scrolling and a cartouche interspersed with elaborate leafage and floral swags, in the same sharp contrast of styles. It is an excellent piece of workmanship in a curiously composite mode.

One of the most characteristic uses of the *appliques* of this period is on the superb writing desks which were and are worth a fortune. Their metal mounts in the Louis XV manner, triumphed in the branched lights springing from their upper corners. The typical support for these candle branches was a woman's or cupid's figure or half figure, and the branches, whether for a single candle or multiplied for many candles, took the form of the candelabrum or *applique* of the period.

Lustres à cristaux—crystal chandeliers, were the 18th Century acme of luxury. The beauty of these creations is almost unearthly, like the unexpected loveliness of an ice storm, breaking into prismatic colors on every tree branch in the morning sunlight. While collectors prize the rare examples of earlier periods, *Louis Quinze* crystal *lustres* are the perfection of luxury. So enamored did society become with the dazzling glitter of glass pendants that in the second half of the century they ornamented most chandeliers. While rock-crystal had been used since the Louis XIV period and was occasionally seen in Louis XV and XVI examples, crystal was more general. This designates a superior quality of glass, while rock-crystal is the natural stone and is semiprecious. Crystal is its closest imitator and is of beautiful clarity, while glass is often imperfect and not always clear, especially the early glass of these periods. *Lustres* were of two types: one where the metal frame was completely covered with crystal beads and tubes and hung with pendants and interlacing garlands—the *lustre à lacé;* the other with a bronze frame ornamented more or less elaborately with pendants, festoons, and pyramids—*lustre à tige découverte*. Like the metal chandelier of the day, the stem was built up of vase or urn forms, and balls, or variously shaped knobs, the candle branches supported by a reversed curved bracket reaching the top of the stem, producing that lyre-shaped outline typical of the period.

A superb example of *lustre* (Fig. 48) with crystal-covered frame has the small marguerites set at close intervals to conceal the joints of the short sections of crystal tubing. This tubing is cut in gouges which catch the light and add to the brilliance of the piece as do

48. Bronze and crystal *lustre*, the frame entirely glassed. Typical lyre-shaped supports ascend to form a spraying corona; daisies top the variously shaped large pendants. Courtesy Bagués, Inc.

the marguerites. From the lyre-shaped supports spring two tiers of candle brackets which end in neat little metal jar-shaped nozzles, below which are set very large saucer-shaped crystal *bobèches* edged with deep scallops. Within these lyre-shaped brackets gleams a large ball and other ornaments, cut to add to the general brilliancy. The *lustre* is topped by the out-curving ends of the brackets forming a broad bouquet which crowns the piece. From this crown and from the brackets depend the large flat leaf-like pendants which are cut in many shapes like the leaves on many trees, each attached by its daisy. The graciousness of these conceptions in crystal is beyond all comparison paramount. Other *lustres* have a central baluster stem like the older models although the lyre-shaped frame is added.

The *lustre à console* stood on a console side table, in place of a *candélabre* or *girandole*. The crystals were either of glass, often Bohemian, or the semiprecious rock-crystal. The variety of shapes in the festoons, spires, and pendants were attractive elements.

Lanterns were often capped by scrolled metal-work reminiscent of the earlier coronas; some had tiny lanterns at the corners, suggesting the older corner turret of Italy and Spain; others followed older forms but were decorated with typical *Régence* ornament. *Lustres* still had the baluster shaped shaft with urn and vase forms and scrolled candle branches; designed with many a whimsey.

The intimate *salon* of the day, the bedroom used as a daytime reception room for both courtiers and ladies, the jolly quality of the work—the caprice and laugh behind it all, explain it. It is as if a master played at work, to please his own whim. But a method underlay all this seeming madness. Whatever the material: wood; metal—bronze, copper, iron, steel, tin, pewter, silver, gold; porcelain from China; colored flowers *de Saxe*—Dresden, or white blossoms, even blue and white from Vincennes; all yielded to the design which dominated the material. Even iron abandoned itself to ribbon bow-knots and was scalloped into flower petals as tiny as any twisted by a little French milliner. It was colored too, like a flower garden, but delicately, not crudely. The style was the thing. Artists and craftsmen alike snapped their fingers in the face of the most stubborn material and forced it into line with the style, while they laughed at both tradition and difficulties and produced excellent and practical lighting fixtures that are in themselves real *objets d'art*.

CHAPTER VI

LOUIS XVI

THINGS in "quiet taste" followed the riot and extravagance of Rococo ornament even before the end of the long reign of Louis XV. For excavators had started to dig up Herculaneum and Pompeii and had brought out into the Italian sunlight those exquisite household objects of ancient days, so full of repose and quiet loveliness that artists forgot self-expression and caprice, and refreshed their spirits at the open spring of classic beauty. Another Renaissance spread over Europe and, by way of England, reached us in America, here inspiring those stately homes of pseudo-classic mold so typical of our early Republic.

France, already secure in her position of dictator as to the etiquette of the world, took the lead as advocate of this new fashion in art. Approved by the Court the new classic—neo-classic style, is known to us as *le style Louis Seize* (1774–1793), although neither Louis nor his queen Marie-Antoinette did more than accept, albeit with some graciousness, that which the artists offered them. The restless caprices of the later Rococo interiors grew stately and calm under this new inspiration, and with the straightening and balancing of chair legs and table legs, lighting fixtures also fell into alignment and took on classic form and ornament. But far from the splendor and splurge of Renaissance forms in the days of *François I* and of *Henri II*, they glorified the beauty of minutia and detail.

Candlesticks, candelabra, *girandoles*, chandeliers, wall brackets, all conformed to classic type and bore none but classic ornament. *Bronze doré* was still the popular material and characteristic of the period. *Ormolu* had a heavier coat of gold than either *bronze doré* or *cuivre doré* and was used from the days of Louis XIV to those of the Empire. It was a hazardous process but the result was lasting and sumptuous. Silver and gold, copper and bronze, iron,

pewter, and tin, glass and porcelain, enamel, and delicate colorings, all were pressed into service in modeling the new forms.

It is a point of some interest to see how the metal workers held
to what the French call the "moral" rule which dictated that gold
should be worked with very great finesse, silver with somewhat
less finesse and more vigor, and bronze with force as well as vigor
and splendid action. These rules held throughout all France as an
established tradition until the Empire period, when the actual
metal ceased to dictate the character of its workmanship and silver
was as finely worked as gold. While in the *Louis Quinze* period all
materials were forced to conform to design, which was paramount,
still the method of working out this design retained these traditions regarding the fineness and spirit of the work. There were over
600 goldsmiths at the time of the French Revolution, not including those enjoying special privilege or attached to the Court. But
so general was the Revolutionary destruction of gold and silver
plate that candlesticks and candelabra of the preceding periods are
of great rarity and exceedingly difficult to obtain.

As in *le style Louis Quinze*, the favorite material for the lighting fixture was *bronze doré*, not infrequently *argenté*, sometimes
vert antique, brun, or even *bleu*—blue. Silver was the mode for
the dining-table and in great houses for other purposes, especially
appliques, candélabres, surtouts de table, and *flambeaux*. The
cuivre doré of the so-called "copper age," when the silver plate of
the realm went into coinage for war, was succeeded at this time
by a much freer use of silver in lighting fixtures, but the appro-
priateness of bronze, and for added decorative effect, rock-crystal,
glass, porcelain, pottery, and precious marbles, was commonly
recognized by both artists and craftsmen. Bronze was cast and then
chiseled and gilded so that sharp delicate decorative ornament
could be worked into the design. The handling of the acanthus leaf
and scrolling is characterized by that little bending of the tips of
leaves—a sort of wilted tip, which gives an inimitable softness and
suavity to the design.

The decorative motifs ornamenting all types of fixtures include
the three decorative influences of the period: the revived Pompei-

ian—known as the neo-classic, or pseudo-classic—false classic; the pastoral or bucolic which diverted the Court of Louis XVI; and *le mode chinoise* which gained a great vogue at this time as the *chinoiserie*. Classic form and ornament were evident in all kinds of fixtures, and, besides the decorative motifs noted, made free use of reeding, fluting, gadrooning, and other conventional ornament as well as ivy and laurel, goats' heads and cupids. Chinese influence was evident where rare Chinese porcelains were mounted in metal-work, or where the metal-work itself showed Chinese ornament, such as figures and pagodas skillfully incorporated in a pastoral or rustic ensemble. The pastoral influence was most pronounced in the more fantastic designs of floral bouquets with porcelain flowers for *appliques* and *girandoles* and for the *mise en scène* of porcelain figures and fowl.

The lure of the out-of-doors spares neither kings nor emperors. Picnicking at the *Petit-Trianon* was an artificial affair at its best, with ribbons and laces, satins, and curls. We are reminded of China's late Empress as she took the air in her palace grounds. More stately and less giddy is the Chinese poetical cult of out-doors; but a *chef* with his retinue must follow an Empress and serve an appropriate meal anywhere her Imperial whim might call a halt. Marie-Antoinette and her dairymaid's milk pail, swung nonchalantly on the very edge of the crater of the French Revolution, fall into the picture with the same pretty irrelevance as does the Chinese Empress with her suite ceremoniously lunching in her palace grounds, refusing to admit that such underlings as the Chinese populace could disturb her honorable Manchu Dynasty.

Lighting fixtures remained as integral a part of the decorative scheme during the reign of *Louis Seize* as in *le style Louis Quinze*. Chandeliers were indispensable. Wall-lights flanked overmantels. But the movable lights became veritable *bijoux*—little gems, as precious as jewels because of their fineness of design and execution. Oil and its possibilities tantalized the thoughts of men; for the resources of multiplied candle-light had been exhausted as long ago as the days of Louis XIV. While the oil lamp was not yet admitted to high society, Argand had invented his burner which, to increase combustion, made use of a double air current and produced a light for which students and night workers were to bless his name during nearly a hundred years, until gas and electricity exceeded all men's expectations. Lamps were still somewhat ungainly things, endeavoring to incorporate classic urn and vase forms into their necessarily mechanical structure.

Flambeaux were the intimate things of life, and as beautiful and chaste as the lines of classic column and other symmetrical baluster forms could make them, in silver, *bronze doré* or *argenté*, marble, alabaster, and especially in porcelain, which was much in fashion because of the increasing vogue for things Chinese. The *monstre* was a low candlestick with socket in the form of a classic urn set on an abruptly cut-column which rested on a round or a square base. Sometimes the column was surmounted by its capital on which the candle socket was placed; the column itself was often nicely fluted, each fluting if in a marble column often being ornamented with that little motif in bronze which the French call *d'asperge*—asparagus. Baluster, column, vase, and human figures vied with each other in fixtures. Artists made free use of lovely half figures, busts, or heads on pedestals in the classic mode. Classic urns and vases made practical candle nozzles; bases were round or square, solid or on paw feet. Classic motifs decorated all types of fixtures: swags, wreaths, eagles, lions, griffins, masks, and even the sphinx of Egypt appeared before the Revolution and Napoleon's Egyptian campaign emphasized its use.

The *bout de table* was charmingly conceived. Some had a tiny low vase-like socket on an abbreviated bit of column and tiny base; or, if a little higher and for two lights, a longer section of column supported a classic vase and from either side the column sprang candle branches. The *chandelier à abat-jour*—a shaded candlestick, grew in importance until it later became typical of the Empire period. Larger candlesticks were made for ecclesiastical use in neo-classic forms of *bronze doré*, silver, and carved and gilded wood, but they lack the majesty of earlier Renaissance models, especially those in silver. The silver hanging altar lamps of the period were more successful but were reserved strictly for church and chapel and not domesticated.

The distinction between the *candélabre, flambeau,* and *girandole* was not at this time very sharply drawn. A *flambeau* similar to the taller *bout de table* might have three lights; a *girandole* three or four; while the *candélabre* was distinguished from the *girandole* either by its larger size or greater number of candle branches. A *candélabre* was a piece of some importance, often of white marble and *bronze doré,* the marble used as base and column or classic vase, and the bronze for draped classic figures and candle branches. Apollo and Daphne, bacchantes, and other mythological figures were favorites either in bronze or porcelain. The typical *candélabre* was that of *bronze, brun*—brown, or *doré,* in the form of a draped or semi-nude woman holding branches which were either natural sprays of blossoming lilies and buds, the candle sockets embedded in the flowers, or were cornucopias with branches. The cornucopia or trumpet-shaped candle socket, so popular during the Empire, was often used at this time. Some *candélabres* were frankly the ancient tripod of Roman days supporting a branched candelabrum. One with hoof feet on a triangular base terminates in three eagle's heads and upholds nine candle branches. Another popular form was a classic vase on a square pedestal set up on bun feet, the vase filled with a bouquet of tulips, the candle nozzles concealed in the blossoms. But the figures of one or two women upholding a blossoming lily branch with nine candle sockets are possibly most typical.

Falconet the noted 18th Century French sculptor had popularized a certain type of nymph. This nymph is frequent in the candelabra of the day. One very fine pair (Fig. 49), each for three candles, has this figure in *bronze brun,* upholding a graceful *ormolu* spray of lilies and tulips much taller than herself. The lily spray is upright, of Easter lily type, the middle terminal blossom concealing a candle socket. On either side of the main stalk, branches a tulip spray with bud and blossom, each blossom concealing a socket. The nymph stands on a pedestal cut in the

form of a short section from a round column. This is ringed at
its base by a reeded *ormolu* molding, and placed on a square flat
base of dark colored marble. This contrast of dark or light marbles

49. The bronze figures of these *candélabres* are designed after a nymph created
by Falconet. The three candle sockets are concealed in the flowers. Courtesy
French & Co.

with metals pleased the taste of the day and is often seen in
various types of fixtures.

Frequently the *ormolu* floral bouquet was placed in a vase (Fig.
50) in quite a natural fashion. One pair of porphyry vases is
typical. The vase is ovoid, of classic form, set on a bronze stem

which rests on a square nicely molded plinth. Classic ornament
decorates the stem and plinth and reaches in leaf forms like a
calix up onto the body of the vase, which is really the ancient
amphora. A band of bronze work with flowing vine pattern en-
circles its body and a narrow line of bronze beading is set at the

50. Bouquets of natural flowers in *ormolu*, the sockets in the flowers, the
vases of porphyry mounted in *ormolu*. Courtesy Bagués, Inc.

base of its neck. Adjusted to the bronze banding are the two
handles which rise between the horns of a goat's head. This head
is a masterpiece as finely conceived as any work of sculpture.
Another narrow bronze beading edges the plate which fits into the
neck of the vase and supports the bouquet. This is wrought in the
most naturalistic fashion: a tulip overtops it with a candle socket;
on one side is a spray of several carnations and buds, one flower
with a socket; on the other is a spray of roses and buds, one half

opened rose holding the socket. The metal-work is so exquisite it tempts the touch as does a beautiful flower.

Candle branches were variously supported. The figure was occasionally that of a griffin supporting the candelabrum on its head. Some examples were very fancifully designed with leaf scrolling, glass pendants and garlands, mythological figures— griffins, dolphins, and other classic favorites.

Precious marbles especially yellow, black, and white were very fashionable and formed the pedestals and often the ovoid vases. The bronze figures and ornaments were usually *bronze doré* or *vert*—a green finish suggesting the antique, or had the ordinary brown finish. Porcelains, exquisitely painted and mounted in *bronze doré*, were used for candelabra as well as candlesticks.

These porcelain figures were often of a rural or pastoral character, a type made popular by the French Court which played at farming at the *Petit-Trianon*. Much ingenuity was shown in the incorporation of the porcelain ornaments. Italy had her own way of using her *Capo di Monte* figures, often set on a pedestal like a work of art and embowered in foliage; but the French manner was inimitable. While they were ordinarily accessory to the design, like a youth and maiden on a pedestal, the candle branches springing from a rustic background, they were often so incorporated in the design as to be an integral part of it. A pair of *Sèvres* bisque figures—a youth standing beside the stump of a tree and a maiden with her basket, is typical. Each figure has its own square porcelain base which is clasped by a chased *ormolu* ornament at each corner and held firmly into a heavy square molded base of the same metal, ornamented in a formal classic design. Behind each figure springs up a cluster of *ormolu* foliage dividing into three branches and ending in urn-shaped sockets with deep bowl-like *bobèches*.

Another pair (Fig. 51), and these are porcelain ducks possibly from Rouen, incorporates them inextricably in the formal *ormolu* candle branches and the natural reeds. The design is characteristically French in its combination of formal and informal elements.

The *girandole,* so popular on the mantelpiece, also took the tripod form with hoof feet on a triangular base, and mounted on the tripod was a vase usually of some rare marble, holding in contrast to its formal outline a bouquet of naturalistic flowers in *bronze doré*, the candle nozzles secreted in the blossoms. *Flambeaux* were similarly designed. A pair in the King's bedroom in the *Petit-Trianon* is in the form of a vase holding a bouquet of

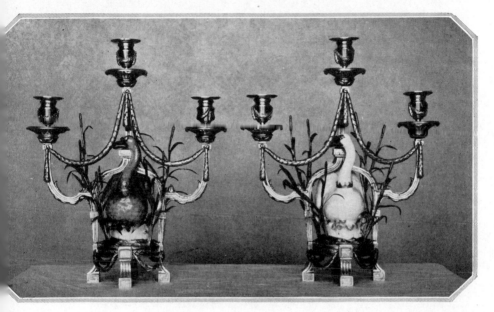

51. Pastoral influence is evident in the treatment of these porcelain ducks mounted in *ormolu*, typical of Rouen work. Courtesy French & Co.

carnation buds, one blossom opening for the candle socket, the flowers realistically wrought.

The *cassolette* was an ingenious contrivance. It was a mantel or console ornament usually in the form of an ovoid vase mounted on a bronze tripod set on hoof feet or griffins. These *cassolettes* were in pairs and, with a clock and a pair of *flambeaux*, formed the accepted *garniture de cheminée*. When extra candle-light was needed on festive occasions, the marble vase covers of the *cassolettes* were taken off and turned upside down, the under side of each being fitted with a candle nozzle. *Flambeaux* were similarly made so that a branched arrangement could be inserted in the candle socket or the socket removed and multiple candle branches put in its place, thus transforming a simple candlestick into an elaborate candelabrum. Such a piece was usually of silver. Venice had used the idea as early as the 15th Century.

Appliques, bras de lumière, were essentials in the interior decorative schemes. They abandoned the irregular forms of the Rococo for the prevailing symmetrical outline. The back or wall-plates were elongated in varying shapes: the classic pedestal was a favorite; quivers filled with feather-tipped arrows or classical motifs variously combined; a *cabochon,* or shield, might be topped by a circle and bow-knot of ribbon and draped with laurel festoons. Vase forms were not uncommon as finials, resting in a nest of acanthus leaves, below which were entwined festoons or an elaborate composition including acanthus, patera—oval or disk, mask, and drapery. The candle branches sprang in dignified curves from these beautiful uprights and terminated in highly sophisticated designs for nozzle and *bobèche,* usually some variant of a classic urn unless the design were floral when great ingenuity was used in secreting the candle sockets within the blossoms. Such conceptions were commonly worked out in enameled metal with porcelain flowers and leaves in soft natural colorings, while the more formal *appliques* were in silvered or gilded bronze and might make use of any motif, even a stag's head and oak leaves.

The composite character of the designs is as notable in some *appliques* as in the *candélabres.* One in silver (Fig. 52), of superlative workmanship, has three branches. The backplate is short and solid looking, composed of a square member, the three sides of which are ornamented with three raised circular paterae. From the middle patera springs a tripartite acanthus leafage finely wrought, and from this spring the formal candle branches. The side branches end in a sharp bend terminated by large sockets, the *bobèche* is *tassa*-shaped—like a low stemmed bowl, and the socket itself a simple cylinder. In contrast to this formal backplate, candle branches, and sockets, the acanthus leafage, the garland,

and the bow-knot are wrought naturalistically. The sharp chisel-
ing of the ornament contrasts intentionally with the suave model-

52. This silver *applique* is finely wrought; its design a composite of classic
elements with the prevalent bow-knot motif. Courtesy French & Co.

ing of the rounded surfaces in the design and furnishes a notable
example of this style.

An *applique* designed by Delafosse (Fig. 53) and signed by the

53. Typical use of classic urn, festoon, and acanthus, with woman's mask and
drapery on the backplate. Courtesy French & Co.

ciseleur Pagot is of *ormolu,* and the best quality of that inimitable gilding. It is a fine example of a type much used since this period. The long wall-plate is ornamented by a mask from which depends formal drapery ending in acanthus and berry finial. A flaming urn tops this wall-plate. A floral garland links the three subtly curved candle branches and they are tipped by leaf-adorned urns and

54. An *applique* in finely chiseled *ormolu* embodies an ovod vase, women's masks, garlands, and acanthus in its characteristic ornament. Courtesy French & Co.

widely accented saucer *bobèches.* Another (Fig. 54) and quite a popular model in finely chased *ormolu* has a very long ovoid vase motif for backplate, hung from long ribbons looped about an ornamental nail-head. The base is highly ornate, a bit finicky except in its right *milieu,* topped by a floral bouquet, and decorated with masks and swags. The ringed and reeded candle arms are formal in contrast, the middle ones spirally reeded. Each ends in a cornucopia-shaped *bobèche* in which are placed plain circular candle sockets edged with small moldings; waterleaves follow the curve of the outer arms from their beaded rings, and end in an outer scroll, while below is a large elaborately foliated scrolling.

Wood was handled no less decoratively. One *applique* is almost completely formed of acanthus and grape foliage, and hung with bunches of grapes. The slender elegant backplate depends from a three-looped bow-knot and the ribbon ends below with tiny tassels. The candle branches start at the bottom of the plate and swing upward in narrow lyre-form. They cross, and then curve outward and upward, supporting gadrooned urn sockets and *bobèches*. An-

55. An *applique* with a backplate of carved and gilded wood, and the candle branches of iron, suggests earlier models. Courtesy Bagués, Inc.

other *applique* (Fig. 55) with carved wood backplate has three iron branches: each *bobèche* outlined by a small corona with its lower edge only indented. The wall-plate has a formal broad rectangular plinth-like member latticed and edged with a molding. A classic acanthus ornament finishes it below and another one on top supports a bouquet of naturalistic roses and leaves in conventional arrangement. It smacks of older forms and earlier times, but is unmistakably *Louis Seize*.

So are the more frivolous floral *appliques* like those of Dresden porcelain (Fig. 56). One of *ormolu* in the shape of a long swaying stalk of Easter lilies, three feet six inches high, with many blos-

soms and buds towering above three similar short sprays ending
in candle sockets. Another is the last word in floral elaboration.
It is from the king's palace in Monza and incorporates Dresden
porcelain flowers in great profusion of kinds and coloring. Its wall-
plate is topped by a bow-knot, the ribbons depending its full
length and ending in two long tassels. The two candle arms bear
tulip cups and the *bobèches* are wide-spreading marguerites; a
fantasy crying aloud for taffetas and brocades, lacquers and lace,
perfumes and pomades.

56. The Dresden porcelain flowers and ribbons are all softly colored in this
applique. Courtesy French & Co.

A charming *lustre* (Fig. 57) with a baluster stem of vase and
basin-shaped members has a profusion of S-scrolled *ormolu* candle
branches supporting small urn-shaped sockets with small flat
bobèches; these branches are lightly hung with crystal garlands
and large faceted pendants. From depending scrolls, high on the
stem, long strands of small crystals are draped to join the candle
branches; and the stem is topped by a graceful bouquet-like scrolling, garlanded from scroll to scroll with a flower-like fringed motif
above.

Hanging lights were never more beautiful than at this time.

Glass and crystal *lustres* were the favorites. These were often slender and graceful in form with long delicate pendants. One in a

57. An exquisite *lustre* of finely chased *ormolu* gracefully hung with crystal festoons and pendants. The central shaft is prominent as in metal chandeliers. Courtesy French & Co.

Fontainebleau salon is topped by a small circlet of this slender pendant fringe below which are draped strings of oblong shaped bits of glass alternating with broader ribbon-like festoons com-

VII. A masterpiece of the art of the *ciseleur*, from the main stairway of the *Musée de Compiègne*. It would cost a fortune to reproduce the perfect detail of trophies and other ornaments. Courtesy Bagués, Inc.

posed of small glass tubing set crosswise. These festoons spread to the large circlet from which the simple candle branches curve outward, and below which strings of glass form a bowl-like bottom ending in the same long delicate fringe of pendants as above, with a single long pendant beneath. The whole effect is simple, delicate, and charming, not fussy or involved. Another *Fontainbleau* example of bronze and crystal has two tiers of trumpet-like candle branches, and is festooned gayly but delicately, with a bouquet effect above and garlands below. Cupids, flaming torches, and other decorative motifs were incorporated in the designs which might include large ornamental glass *bobèches*. At this period the *bobèche* was often accented in such a way as to give special character to the candle socket.

Lanterns abandoned the caprices of the Louis XV style for cylindrical and other simple rectangular or polygonal forms surrounding a more or less elaborate chandelier with close clustering branches. The metal framework and scrolled supports were minutely ornamented with the same care that characterized all the metal-work of the period.

To reproduce one of these superb cylindrical lanterns to-day would cost a fortune. Elaborated in minute detail, the work on these *bronze doré* lanterns is a thing of marvel. One which hung on the main stairway of the *Musée de Compiègne* (Fig. VII) is crowned with trophies or horns and ropes, arrows and torches, and has two of the sauciest cupids imaginable perched inside above its many deeply curved candle branches. It is a masterpiece of a lifetime, possible only to a great artist craftsman. These lanterns incased cylindrically with glass were the glory of the period.

If of *tôle* the designs were far less formal, but had some dignity however ornamental. The framework in one example (Fig. 58) is of plain strapping, relieved here and there with a scalloped edge; the body hexagonal; the roof in an elongated point, terminating in a cupola; hung round with long cones like little bells. At each top corner of the panels and in the middle of each of their lower edges are bouquets of flowers and leaves. When painted in the soft delicate colorings peculiar to *le style Louis Seize* these *tôle* lanterns were far from inelegant. The framework was usually plain, and was ornamented with natural bouquets of flowers. The

58. A *tôle* lantern decked in colored flowers, the frame and flowers painted in soft colorings. Courtesy Bagués, Inc.

principal interior use of lanterns was in the vestibule, hall, or stairway.

CHAPTER VII

DIRECTOIRE AND EMPIRE

Iт might be expected that a Revolution so sanguinary and awful as that of the French in the 18th Century would not only disturb but would fairly uproot art, so that it would have to be replanted if it were to flourish at all. But nothing of the sort took place. There is scarcely a break in the quiet, orderly development of the classic style, which appeared in the late years of the reign of Louis XV, and developed into *le style Louis Seize,* only to run its course in the Directoire and Empire.

Lighting fixtures testify to this as plainly as do other objects that embellished the home, so that far from revealing any gap in French period styles, the products of the late 18th and early 19th Centuries would have been classed as Louis XVII had an aristocrat been still in the saddle instead of the Little Corporal. But under a king there would naturally have entered into the work of the Court artists, Percier and Fontaine, a greater suavity and graciousness, with less need for the self-assertion and over-emphasis upon the force of his imperial régime which Napoleon felt necessary to convince the masses. All this appears in the designs of French lighting fixtures, and in their character we may read much of the history of the time.

Percier and Fontaine were the imperial architects, and to them we owe the lighting fixture designs which carried out their interior schemes in strict conformity to a coördinated plan, as was done by the Adam Brothers in England. The term Directoire has been given to the style of work produced by Percier, Fontaine, and others, during the period when Napoleon was a member of the Directorate, and for convenience has been used to cover the short term of the Consulate which preceded the Empire. The splendid lighting fixtures which officially added to the pomp and ceremony of Napoleon's Court were doubtless designed by Percier, as Fontaine confined himself to architecture. In these designs we detect little of the ugly and the crude, the over-burdening of ornament, and that blatant quality often charged against the Empire style as a whole. This fact is largely due to the great state of perfection achieved by the metal workers of the period. Bronze, cast and chiseled by the *ciseleurs*, and finely gilded—*doré* or *ormolu*, was the height of their achievement in this direction.

In Directoire models there are lovely classical fixtures that seem to have evolved naturally from *Louis Seize* types. *Flambeaux, candélabres, appliques, bras de lumière* or *appliques, lustres*, and *lanternes* all are symmetrical and graceful but abandon some of the ease and whim of the *Louis Seize* models, retain the sphinx and eagle, and encourage more purity of style in classic reproduction. Directoire construction and ornament retained a certain graciousness, slender proportions, some delicacy, but added a sureness of outline, a clean-cut effect whose emphasis in *le style Empire* became more rigid and more conventional.

The *applique* received minute attention, and was designed with that precision typical of classic outline and ornament. A good example (Fig. 59) is of *bronze doré* varied with a contrasting *vert antique*. The wall-plate is oval, with its outline varied at top in a slight lip turning outward from the wall. It is nicely modeled in a quite individual handling of acanthus leaves. Is it clear that an artist's use of the classic acanthus leaf or the anthemion, often called the honeysuckle ornament, is individual and far from wearisome? This fact is never more apparent than in this late revival of classic design. While Directoire and Empire designs are of classic inspiration they are not mere reproductions, and delight by the very individuality which distinguishes their ornament from *Louis Seize*, Renaissance, or classic models. This fact is evident in this bronze *applique*. The serpent is handled with the minute care bestowed by Egyptians on their beautiful gold jewelry; every scale is delicately but decisively formed. Its head curves outward from the ring in which it is coiled, to support one of the side candle cups; and its tail curves outward similarly to support the opposite one. The coil itself supports the middle

socket. In the use of Directoire material for furnishings, the possibilities of Egyptian form and ornament should not be neglected,
as they did not wait upon Napoleon's Egyptian campaign to
make their appearance in France; although artists under his imperial patronage later emphasized them. The candle cup here
used suggests a floral calix or conventionalized blossom, with row
upon row of overlapping petals. The whole effect is that of neat-
ness and fineness sufficient to please the most fastidious taste.

59. *Applique* of the Directoire Period with the characteristic twisted serpent in
vert antique and the fixture *bronze doré*. Courtesy Bagués, Inc.

A charming *ormolu* Directoire *lustre* (Fig. 60) makes use of
two rather chubby cupids perched confidently on the rim of the
central vase motif, from which they are stepping off with a hardi-
hood scarcely warranted by their lack of wings. Each holds aloft
a double horn, curving in an S-shape out and up, to hold two
candles thus adding an upper tier of four lights to the eight
candles on the lower tier of branches. The chandelier itself is
formed of a broadly shaped classic urn with a short neck. Four
chains suspend it from a small canopy above. Upon the neck of
this urn the *amours* are marching, and between them a staff with
a classic bud finial reaches more than half-way up toward the
canopy, giving a note of definition and finish to the design. The
vase is beautifully ornamented in classic banding and other motifs,
and completed by a long berry finial. The deeply C-scrolled

branches are attached to the rim of its body. They end in delicately expanding trumpet or cornucopia tops into which are set the short tubular candle cups. The surface of the lower branches is minutely decorated, and the sharpness of their outline broken by leaf-tips

60. This *ormolu lustre* (1795–99) in *le style Directoire*, more delicately shaped than the Empire models is formed of a suspended classic vase supporting dancing cupids blowing uplifted trumpets. Courtesy The Metropolitan Museum.

and scrolls in typical Directoire fashion. This *lustre* was doubtless made between the years 1795–99. A point to note in its composition is the lamp form frequently used during the Renaissance period especially in the hanging sanctuary lamps of Italy and Spain. In the cult of the classic prevailing at this period, we may expect to find a revival of the Roman lamp motif which forms the basis of the typical Empire metal chandelier, as it does of the shallow bowl-like bottom of the crystal *lustre*.

The famous bronze workers, Gouthière and Thomire, noted for their accomplishment under the old régime, were logically the leaders under the Directoire and the Empire. Gouthière was what the French call a *"ciseleur délicieux, spirituel et tendre,"* ever working with the forms of women and cupids. Thomire abandoned such sweetness as clung to the work of Gouthière even under the Empire, for the sharper definition of classic Roman work.

A pair of *flambeaux* (Fig. 61) in a typical Thomire design is of *bronze doré*. In this candlestick a not too chubby cupid, with good serviceable wings, stands at some ease on a circular pedestal, which curves fluently into a spreading base edged with beading and set on a circular plinth of the same width. He bears directly on his head a tall beautifully woven basket filled with flowers which he steadies with one hand. These flowers surround the half-concealed candle socket. This was a type much in vogue and often used by designers. It is a variant of the *chandelier à personnage* of earlier days which grew in favor with the Empire period. Human or mythological figures, animals, birds, or chimerical creatures were ever in evidence.

Napoleon's Egyptian campaign lent an excuse for a freer use of the sphinx, the lotus, and the palm. The emphasis of his imperial power inclined designers to choose warlike decorative motifs—the Phrygian helmet, saber, thunderbolt, shield, laurel, bay, wreath, torch, cornucopia, wings, serpents, lions' and bears' claws; to these were added the Greek fret, anthemion, acanthus, and pineapple; with wiverns and other chimerical beasts.

Flambeaux were of five types: column or baluster, classic or Egyptian; tripod; figure—woman, cupid, satyr, etc., supporting a candle socket; classic ovoid vase; or *carquois*—quiver-shaped, the shaft expanding to a broader lip like a modern flower vase. Bases were molded in various forms, usually round. Sockets were concealed in shafts or vases, or were individual classic urns set on the stems or borne on the heads of figures. A baluster stem with

three or four human heads below a classic urn and as many pairs of
feet set on the large molded base below, suggesting that the figures

61. *Flambeau* with a basket of fruit used as a *bobèchon* upheld by Cupid;
typical of Thomire's designs. Empire; *bronze doré*. Courtesy Bagués. Inc.

were bound within the shaft, was not an uncommon motif, hinting
of Egyptian mummies.

One of the most significant elements in Empire *flambeaux* and
candélabres was the use of human figures in the rôle of servants or
slaves holding the lights. The candelabrum was either balanced on

the head of a human figure, a satyr, griffin, or other chimerical animal, or a human figure held a crown or circlet supporting the lights, held a staff, a cornucopia, or the scrolled branches themselves in one or both hands. In the *grand salon* at *Malmaison* is a pair of *candélabres* each of which has the winged figure of a woman poised on a sphere upholding with both hands a laurel wreath from which spring seven candle branches forming a coronet. These *candélabres* stand on the mantelpiece, as part of a *garniture* with a pair of porcelain vases of Etruscan form made at *Sèvres* in 1806. A pair of figures, that of a man and a woman, might be used for a pair of *candélabres*. Large classic urns were borne on the heads of draped figures. Some *candélabre* shafts were of reeded columns or the Roman fasces, emblem of the lictors' authority. A *candélabre* at *Fontainebleau* has the shaft topped by a plumed helmet, with flags stacked below, two tiers of candle branches, the whole set on a tall plinth with broader base supported by tortoises—truly a worthy foundation of ancient days.

The candle socket was greatly varied. Candlesticks either concealed the socket or emphasized it in the form of a beautiful rounded classic urn, occasionally polygonal like some examples at *Fontainebleau*. In these the *bobèche* was seldom accentuated, usually being the base of the urn itself. Candelabra and chandeliers made even greater use of the cornucopia or trumpet form with or without an extra socket. It often suggests the lotus capital of Egyptian columns. Occasionally we find one bent in a reversed curve, as in the preceding periods, but they usually spring abruptly outward and upward from the shaft of a candelabrum or chandelier. The floral *bobéchon*—candle socket, was also taken from the preceding period. Bases varied greatly; cut-columns supported human or animal figures or were topped by spheres or half spheres on which the figures were poised. The triangular classic plinth having cut corners either with or without feet was popular. Rectangular tapering bases were common. White and dark marble, especially dark veined marble, was favored. The marble bases were often finely decorated with applied metal ornament: draped figures, festoons, wreaths, etc.

As the monumental candelabrum was the piece of greatest importance at the time of the Roman Empire and the Italian Renaissance, so the French Empire saw the apotheosis of the candelabrum in France. It took on majestic heights and became an important factor in decoration, whether standing on floor, table, mantelpiece, or pedestal. Artists expended as great care in candelabrum designing as upon important sculpture; and the *ciseleurs* were no whit behind them in carrying out their designs in the actual metal. Whether or not we are great admirers of *le style Empire* we must commend the splendid metal-work of this period. It was, as has since been proved, the last word in the art of the metal worker. Whatever finish was chosen, whether a *patine brun* or *noire*—black, *bleu, doré,* or *vert antique,* each fits the subject with the peculiar exactitude of the antiquarian. There it is—a splendid cult of the antique. The term *candélabre* was also applied to the tall carved and gilded wooden pedestal or *torchère* of Roman type, or to an elaborate large piece with two branched arms, for the corner of a *salon,* on which *candélabres* or *girandoles* were placed.

A pair of figures (Fig. 62), when upholding single candle sockets, of an ornate and important character, are called *candélabres* by the French instead of *flambeaux.* In this pair the figures stand at rest on circular cut-columns, reversed so that the capital of lotus leaves rests upon a square base. The candle stem is a circular rod, simply ornamented, resting on the column but held upright by the raised arm of the figure. Well above the head the stem expands into a broad *bobèche* whose upturned edges are scalloped. The socket is urn-shaped with a flaring slightly scalloped lip.

One pair (Fig. 63) with a great deal of spirit is made of *bronze doré* mounted on a pedestal of dark marble, again evidencing the taste for contrasting shades and color tones in the ornament of the day. The spirited figures bearing these *candélabres* are stepping forward briskly. The woman holds the *candélabre* aloft in her left hand, the man in his right. The entire composition is of majestic height and the figures, although themselves far from life-size, are modeled with as much care as if they were monumental. Each grasps the central stem of a two-tiered branched candelabrum, the branches curving upward in the Empire style and ending in cornucopias. S-scrolled ornaments near the stem

62. Empire *candélabres*, the cut-column suggesting an Egyptian column reversed, with figures upholding the candle sockets. Bronze. Courtesy Bagués, Inc.

break the severity of the curves. The figures are mounted on rectangular bronze plinths with cut corners set on similarly shaped marble bases. The entire pedestal is formed of a sort of double base, separated by moldings, the lower one much the larger. Both bases are of dark veined marble, the bronze molding covered with ornament. Classic applied figures and garlands decorate the upper pedestal. These are magnificent pieces and enough to convert any

63. Very large Empire *candélabres* for fifteen candles each, of *bronze doré* on pedestals of dark veined marble; the upper pedestals ornamented by classic figures and swags in applied metal-work. Courtesy The Metropolitan Museum.

one however reluctant to give full due to the work of the Empire period.

Although Napoleon had been responsible for the destruction of the incomparable silver-work long treasured in Spain, his designers made free use of silver in the candle fixtures for his imperial table, and set the fashion for France. One fine *candélabre* of the period (Fig. 64) has a circular stem, pinching in as it joins the domed base. It bears an ovoid vase whose neck holds the tubular

64. A superb silver *candélabre* in the Empire style with typical acanthus scrolled cornucopia candle branches terminating in beautiful swans. Made for Napoleon in the hundred day period between his return from Elba and his final exile to St. Helena. Courtesy Cartier.

socket. From the body of the vase four cornucopia branches spring in the familiar C-curve typically Empire. Into their wide mouths fit tubular candle sockets. A slender elaborately voluted acanthus scroll turns backward from each branch, and a swan with lowered neck is placed at the juncture of branch and vase.

The term *girandole* was still somewhat confused with *candélabre,* but generally it referred to a small *candélabre* as formerly.

Biennais, the silversmith, made beautiful three-branched *giran-doles* for Napoleon. His *cassolettes* of silver were no less hand-some. He also made *grandes chandeliers*—great candlesticks, for the altar, employing the motif of the eagle or the Hapsburg double-headed eagle at their bases.

Thomire usually executed Percier's designs in silver and bronze. His gilded metal was superb and he was noted for his lighting fixtures and clocks. Auguste and Biennais dominated all the work in silver plate during the imperial epoch. Biennais made many *candélabres, torchères,* and *garnitures de cheminée.* Auguste made the noted *surtout de table* presented to Napoleon by the City of Paris. The *surtout de table* lent great state and dignity to the banqueting table at this time, and became an elaborate and cere-monious affair. The *surtout* made by Auguste as a gift to Napoleon from Charles IV of Spain, was of *pierre dure*—different colored marble, alabaster, agate, porphyry, cameos, etc., and *bronze doré.* It consisted of thirty-one pieces. Twenty-two of these formed *candélabres* with three or four lights each. Nine of the pieces represented temples, fountains, and altars. They were mounted on *bronze doré* and were ornamented with statues and bas reliefs.

One very interesting fixture (Fig. 65) which came into use dur-ing the Empire period, shows clearly the origin of the modern lamp with its large circular shade. It is a *candélabre* with closely set candle branches placed either high or low on an upright; the base, candle branches, and big flaring adjustable metal shade decorated with ornament in the style of the period. An arrow or sort of key adjusts the shade. This fixture was for candles, however.

Possibly the most noted change in the wall fixtures was the motif of the arrow supporting the candle socket horizontally, although arrows had been incorporated in earlier models but not conspicuously. One example of *bronze ciselé et doré* has four arrows fixed in a circular medallion as if each had been shot into a target. But not all *appliques* showed as radical a change, although the downward pointing arrow was a favorite device for the wall-plate. In some the feather tip became a formal anthemion, below which might be a rayed mask of the sun, and below this four upward curving trumpets for candle sockets. A flaming torch was also a favorite backplate. But the lyre form, bow-knots, and cupids were not abandoned. In *Fontainebleau* is a finely shaped backplate in the form of a lyre, the top with two out-

65. It is easy to trace the evolution of the modern lamp with its large circular shade to this Empire *candélabre* with its close-set candle branches. Bronze. Courtesy The Metropolitan Museum.

curving eagles' heads from whose beaks hang crystal festoons. An anthemion crests the piece, and festoons of small crystals drape it at even intervals, with a few delicate long pendent drops to add grace. The entire form is slender and beautiful. The five candle branches are conventionalized urns with somewhat accentuated *bobèches*. A half figure of a winged victory, cupid, or some chimerical creature emerging from acanthus ornament and upholding candle branches, was a characteristic design for the pairs of *appliques* which were as integral a part of the interior decorative schemes as in the preceding periods.

66. Cupid plays his part on the stage of this bronze *lustre* topped by a crown of spreading palmettes. Empire. Courtesy Bagués, Inc.

The typical Empire *lustre* was of *bronze doré* and *cristal,* occasionally *cristal de roche,* although elegant examples were made in iron or in bronze alone, variously finished and ornamented with characteristic period motifs.

A bronze *lustre* (Fig. 66) makes conspicuous use of Cupid, in fact exalts him above any former period. While not enthroned, he poises enraptured on the top of the neck of a broadly accentuated vase. The bottom of the vase is shaped like a basin with a large pineapple finial below. It hangs by four ornamental chains from a disk from which depends another pineapple finial, and from whose edges long serrated leaves ascend forming a corona suggestive of earlier models. The four short candle branches are attached to the lower body of the vase, and support small circular *bobèches* and sockets. The sides and bottom of the vase are decorated with applied ornament including fine scrolled cresting and beautifully modeled animal heads.

Another large *ormolu lustre* (Fig. 67) is arranged for twenty candles, whose short reeded cornucopia branches spring from the basin-like bottom of a similar classic vase. Its outline however is much broadened, a typical Empire model. The branches are ringed and leaf-adorned, and the band from which they spring is minutely ornamented. A banding of conventionalized laurel runs below it, and the basin is perfectly gadrooned. Its finial is an acanthus ornament ending in a conventionalized pineapple motif. The candle branches are trumpet-shaped, and are decorated with smooth leaves suggestive of the lotus capitals of Egyptian temples. In each trumpet's mouth is set the practical tubular socket typical of the day. A wave motif edges the basin's rim. The *lustre* is hung by six ornamental chains composed of pierced and solid sections. These depend from a much smaller disk or canopy, from which hangs a large pineapple finial. A corona of formalized palm leaves or palmettes, tops the piece reminiscent of ancient models. The surface of the metal is all carefully ornamented with that excellence of detail which is the great accomplishment of Empire metal-work. But no cupid holds the center of this stage; instead an active flame motif fills the mouth of its broad vase, a favorite element in Empire designs.

Bronze and crystal *lustres* were of several types. The most familiar has a shallow bowl-like bottom formed of strings of small crystals, often *cristaux de Bohême*—Bohemian glass, strung symmetrically—*enfilés,* or alternating with bands of pierced metal-work. In others the corona is hung with festoons draped from the candle branches, giving a lighter effect. One type has three coronas, decreasing in size as they ascend, the whole structure draped

67. A magnificent ormolu *lustre,* the suspended classic lamp aflame and circled with cornucopia candle branches; ornamental chains, and a crown of palmettes. Empire. Courtesy Bagués, Inc.

with crystal strings like a cascade, finished with a crystal fringe and ball pendant. Other examples show the ornamental metal framework with less glass. Some are crested by a crown of palm leaves or palmettes, and finished below by a *pomme de pin*—pineapple.

The oil lamp was still an uncertain affair although it took on the classic vase and urn forms and classic ornament. One highly sophisticated type of *lampe* which appeared, variously decorated, was a small globe which held a wick, the globe suspended from a curved support poised on the head of a figure, perhaps a chimerical creature who sat on a sort of broad basin-topped pedestal. This was set on a fluted stem with a rectangular base on paw feet. This type of *lampe* gave the designer an opportunity to use classic motifs somewhat freely and was a thing of beauty. The term *lampadaire* was used for the monumental candelabrum of Roman type for hanging lamps, with its standard composed of vase and urn motifs, and ornamented with swags, eagles' and goats' heads, winged lions, sphinxes, acanthus, and anthemion. Percier and Fontaine's book of designs includes two lamps in the form of a globe, one surmounted by a classic head, the other by a figure; the oil burners branching at right angles from the globular oil reservoir, the whole contrivance being set upon a beautiful standard of the classic type.

Lanternes of bronze or iron were equally rich and elegant. In *bronze doré* they were essentials for halls, on stairways, and in vestibules, and were also hung from arched openings in great houses or palaces. They were rectangular, many sided, or circular, of Renaissance or Louis XVI type but with the more austere decoration of the Empire period.

A lantern (Fig. 68) of the early 19th Century, originally from the *Tuileries,* is of cast iron and a fine specimen of this type of work which won approval in both Europe and America during the last century. It is circular, receding toward the bottom, and ends with a somewhat elaborate scroll motif below the framing of each of its four panes. Above the panes runs a small well shaped molding and a vertically pierced band. The top molding is crested with spread-eagles perched over the panes, with formal anthemions between them. The slanting top is capped with a small lantern like those of earlier periods. This is pierced and crested with formal scrolled ornaments. The finial is a sphere topped by a flame.

The two points of advancement in lighting were an increasing use of the eye-shade and the fixing of candle branches for convenience to many articles of furniture: small dressing glasses, long mirrors, and secretaries, ink stands, and writing desks were so outfitted; a practical custom which added to the importance and

68. This is one of the magnificent iron *lanternes* from the *Tuileries;* decorated with a flaming crest, spread-eagles, and anthemions; the lantern on typical scrolled supports. Empire. Courtesy French & Co.

dignity of the piece. With the short restoration of the French monarchy under Louis XVIII, less sophistication and a lack of fine workmanship marked many of the fixtures. *Lustres* were more sparsely hung with glass, and the pendants often recurred to the earlier flat shapes suspended from small cut stars or daisies. Artists lacked imperial patronage under the Republic and fixtures of the middle and later 19th Century fell into the mediocre, until the 20th Century awakened to the revaluation of the older period styles and the cult of new art forms.

CHAPTER VIII

EARLY ENGLISH

FIFTEEN centuries must be accounted for between the nights when Rome's Governor burned beautiful Roman lamps in his villa in Britain, and that time when Roman influence returned in the art of the Renaissance and was heartily welcomed by the rich and popular English "King Hal" (1509). So little remains of lighting fixtures made in England before the 17th Century, however, that the few outstanding examples, like the 12th Century Gloucester Candlestick, are the only evidence of what must have been. The Anglo-Saxons were famous metal workers, so famous that they even traveled to Rome and made their decorative lamps in the Imperial City itself. At the time of their conquest by the Normans (1066) they had more gold and silver than France. But the Norman plundering about finished what the Danes had left, and England cast what remained into her own 16th Century melting pot for war; so that the desolations of time are not alone accountable for this dearth of early English lighting fixtures.

During the fifteen centuries preceding the Renaissance, candles of wax and tallow, torches, rushes, and oil lamps gave feeble light to castle and cottage. Their fixtures were decorated in the styles of the successive periods: Anglo-Saxon—pagan and Christian (1st to 11th Centuries), French or Norman Romanesque (1066), Gothic (1189), and Renaissance (1509). While the styles of the earlier decorative periods may seem to have had little influence on later fixtures, still they contributed to that trend which made the later styles differ from those on the Continent, though inspired by them. The Renaissance invasion of foreign artists and craftsmen made slow headway notwithstanding Henry VIII's generous patronage. The masses, just coming out of their Medieval submergence, yielded their beloved Gothic style with characteristic insular slowness.

Copper and bronze were valued metals during the Anglo-Saxon period. Fixtures of the finer sort were of copper, bronze, silver, silver-gilt, doubtless with *champlevé* enamel known from the pre-Roman Celtic period, of carved bone and possibly ivory. Hand candlesticks, used since Roman days, had prickets or sockets. Chandeliers hung in churches and castles. Lamps of Roman type, with wick spout or nozzle, had handles or were hung. The primitive open oil pan, single or double, with a bent corner for the wick, similar to the French *candile,* the Scotch *cruʒie,* and the American Betty and Phœbe lamps, was the common type for humble use until the 17th Century. It could hang or stand, and might have an adjustable ratchet to raise or lower the lamp. This lamp was usually constructed of iron.

Seventh Century metal-work combined copper and silver most decoratively. Metal bowls characteristically ornamented with enameled medallions served as lamps—"Saxon-dishes" they were called. Anglo-Saxon metal workers in Rome in the 8th and 9th Centuries were making these *gabatæ*—lamps, of copper and silver hung on chains, and ornamented with inlay and jewels in foliage and animal patterns, with medallions; adding that divergent motif which later returned to England by way of Ireland. Foliage decoration prevailed from the 11th to the 13th Centuries, but 11th Century figure work was preëminent, and to-day wins praise for its vigor, delicacy, originality, fancy, and technique. If the carved bone candlesticks given to Exeter Cathedral (1050–73) resembled the famous ivory crook handle coming to us from this time, they were indeed works of art. The enormous hands of the figures are characteristic of the period, as is evident on the Gloucester Candlestick (Fig. 69).

In the Norman-Romanesque period, the earlier forms continued in use, as many of them did as late as the 17th Century. Torch holders fixed to the walls, taper holders, candlesticks, hanging fixtures, lamps, and lanterns held the lights. England naturally adopted the styles of her French conquerors, and imported the typical Limoges enameled pricket candlestick, a grease pan on its knopped stem and with tripod feet, or the tall pricket set

directly on its base. The Gloucester Candlestick dating from this
period has this knopped stem, and preserves its type notwithstanding its intricate design in which squirming men, animals,

69. The Gloucester Candlestick of gilt bell-metal, 12th Century, 1 ft. 11 in.
high. Courtesy Victoria and Albert Museum.

and animated scrolling stem-work seem suddenly to have come to a
magic standstill.

So much of the story of English metal-work hangs around this
Gloucester Candlestick that it cannot be given too careful con-

sideration. A highly sophisticated piece of work, it promises much for the work of its immediate period of which little is known. It promises even more for the successive centuries up to the 17th, of which we still have meager knowledge; but of even greater interest to the antiquarian it evidences the accomplishment of the previous centuries. Because a work of such intricacy, even over elaboration, witnesses to the fact of a long period of progressive accomplishment before it could have been either conceived or fabricated. It dates from the year 1110, an ecclesiastical piece, and we cannot be assured that any such elaboration was thought fit or was possible for a home or even for a castle, because English living was of a primitive Medieval sort at this date. It was the period of rush-strewn floors—the so-called "marsh" of the times, and torches held at table by servants. The candlestick is made of white gilded bronze but its quota of silver permits its classification as the work of a silversmith. It is 1 ft. 11 in. high and its base is 8 in. in diameter. Its design embraces forty-two monsters and nine human figures in its continuous scrolled intricacies. As we have written elsewhere of this piece: it is whim carried to the zenith of deliberate intention. French influence is evident in its structural resemblance to the *dinanderie* candlesticks, and Gothic in its scrolling, leaf tips, and trefoils; but above these there are evident earlier native influences, particularly Celtic.

It will repay minute study. While the general outline of the feet has the look of the strutting *dinanderie,* their further ornament emphasizes this concept. Down each of these feet—and they are so high we might even call them legs, down each of them writhes a reptile with the peculiar squirm of its species. The head turns upward expectantly with its ready jaws slightly agape. Balancing this conception at the top of the candlestick, three highly formalized griffins with characteristic beading for their backbones, are crawling upward with their heads just topping the very broad grease pan. It will be noted that in both of the structural elements, feet and grease pan, these chimerical creatures are purely accessory; the structure is complete without them as they perform none but a decorative function. There is an occasional leaf tip ending some scroll, and this is handled with the full curve of Gothic ornament, but more often it is a curious human head.

Candlesticks of this Norman-Romanesque period were made of copper, bronze, pewter, latten, and wrought-iron, occasionally silver-gilt, carved bone, ivory, and rock-crystal. Decorative silverware of these early periods was almost always gilded with water-gilding to prevent tarnishing.

Latten, variously spelled in old English, was a mixture of copper and zinc which is really brass, but the word seems to have been used to include bronze. Plain brass was later silvered or gilded. The English aristocracy spoke French after the conquest and *chandelier* meant a candle-holder whether a candlestick, candelabrum, or hanging chandelier. The name has stuck in the English language though we use it only for the hanging fixture which has long abandoned candles. English fixtures were Continental in type, simplified in ornament by less skillful local craftsmen. Wicks were extinguished and trimmed by hand, and as lamp wicks of hemp, pith, or vegetable fiber needed less snuffing than candle wicks, lamps were used in the chambers of the better homes as well as in kitchen and cottage. Lanterns were used very anciently; called lanthorns, they suggest that translucent sheet of horn which protected the flame and yet gave out some portion of its light. Lanterns were later occasionally made of painted wood. English ironwork was strictly native and followed simple Medieval models until the late 17th Century.

French models continued fashionable in the Gothic period (1189–1509). The pillar, or lobed, candlestick with stem of clustered columns like those of Limoges enamel suggesting the Gothic pillar, was a favorite model. *Dinanderie* work was imported in the 13th Century and was much in vogue. Dinant, a town in Flanders near Liège, was destroyed by *Phillipe le Bon*—though he must have been far from good, in 1466, and the metal workers were dispersed, some of them reaching England and further popularizing the Flemish styles. Candlesticks were often of precious metals, rock-crystal, and ivory, but commonly of copper, bronze, latten, pewter, and iron. The 14th Century vogue for carved ivory in England extended to candlesticks when these were at all costly, as was the tendency at this period, when even bronze and copper were made resplendent by gilding.

Medieval forms in silver were doubtless similar to those in brass and enamel. While no domestic silver plate now exists earlier than the 14th Century, we read of Henry III (1216–72) presenting silver candlesticks to Westminster Abbey, and we can guess at the magnificence of such candlesticks from the elaboration of the earlier one of Gloucester. The typical Gothic candlestick had a stem intersected with knops; foot round, polygonal, or tripod. The column form with square dished plinth was used in the 13th Century. The old English custom of holding auctions "by inch of candle," in use until the late 19th Century, dates from at least the 14th. A candle was divided into one inch sections and whatever was sold went to the last bidder before the flame died out.

Hanging lights were the characteristic Gothic hoop or corona pierced to hold small conical glass oil cups or arranged for candles; or the candle-beam, beams of wood or metal simply crossed, though often gayly painted. When for permanent lighting instead of some special festival illumination, rarely more than one hanging light—hanging candelabrum, was used in a room, and this was thought a luxury even for a palace. These simple Gothic hanging fixtures were in use until supplemented by the more costly imported metal chandeliers with foliated Gothic candle branches and perforated sockets. Hanging lights were occasionally of gold and silver in both corona and branched types. Branched chandeliers were rare, usually for churches, and bore ecclesiastical figures and Gothic ornament.

The 15th Century saw many developments in the crude lighting arrangements of earlier Gothic days. English interiors came more and more to resemble Continental interiors. Candelabra— branched candlesticks in use in the 14th Century, were now made with removable branches, a new idea introduced from Venice. This economic arrangement left a single candlestick for ordinary use, reserving the added branches for festive occasions, a model long popular with silversmiths in France and in England, though English examples are rare before the time of George III. The candelabrum with a dished stand and the branches springing from an upright could be hung up or set on a table. Hanging candlesticks were not uncommon. In the late Gothic period chandeliers were hung both in the great halls and smaller rooms of the house. The life of the family had formerly centered in the common hall, but in the 14th Century a desire for greater privacy brought the use of separate rooms, a tendency which did not become general until the Renaissance. Chandeliers of iron were painted in bright colors and sometimes decorated with enamel, jewels, and gold work. Henry VII had a number of silver chandeliers, some plain silver, some parcel-gilt—partly gilded. None exists however earlier than the Restoration. By the year 1434 eight-branched chandeliers were not unusual and the Continent, especially the Netherlands, continued to supply England with her brass chandeliers until the middle of the 18th Century, though they were never plentiful until the Restoration. Silver basins suggesting the old Saxon lamp or the Italian sanctuary lamp were hung in churches, but these were for candles, and had an inner basin of latten to catch the drippings from their serges—great wax candles. An interesting record dated 1492 notes—"my candylbeme that hangeth in my hall with VI bellys of laton standying thereon." A hanging light was also called a "belle canstyke" and a portable light a "lesser" candlestick.

With the Renaissance the lighting of smaller rooms became a factor in domestic comfort and the English home came into its own. Latten candlesticks were plentiful, and five instead of a pair might occasionally be used in a single room. Gothic designs persisted in iron tripods for rushlights and for pewter and brass candlesticks; but pewter and brass also followed the newer styles of the native silversmiths. The typical candlestick had a circular dished foot, a stem intersected with a wide grease pan, and a more distinct development of the nozzle. Returning from The Field of the Cloth of Gold where Francis I displayed the splendor of France, Henry VIII lavished his patronage on artists and craftsmen from Italy, France, and the Netherlands, and lighting fixtures were made to conform to the growing taste for magnificence. Holbein, John of Padua, Torrigiano, Rovezzano, and Toto del Nunziata were among the foreign artists in England. Holbein the painter, was also an architect and designed furniture. John of Padua was both architect and musician. Toto del Nunziata was largely responsible for Nonesuch Palace built at Cheam about 1541 mostly by foreign artists. Evelyn the delightful diarist, tells us they were Italian, French, and Dutch. Torrigiano had charge of Henry VII's tomb in Westminster.

While exquisite bronze Renaissance candlesticks were imported from Italy and Flanders, all materials were locally used. Silver and silver-gilt was splendidly wrought for candles as big as torches in Woolsey's palace, which at a word he yielded to his king. Great "standinge" candlesticks were made of wood. Some were of iron: one on a square foot with a screw vise; some were gilt and painted with figures of women and cupids in Renaissance style. Rush-light holders were of iron, and these early types remained in use until about 1830 when wax covered rushes were supplanted by other means of lighting. For night lights the rush was placed in a sort of drum for protection. Ceramics were a rarity at this time for few oriental porcelains had yet reached England. Italian maiolica was just approaching its perfection, while local pottery was crude. In an inventory of Henry VIII's are listed four hundred and fifty articles of glass probably Venetian, many of them blue, some partly gilt, others amber. Among these appear "lowe candlesticks," "great bell candlesticks," and "aulter candlesticks." Venetian glass was often elaborately mounted in silver-gilt as was the rare Chinese porcelain, and Continental and English pottery, evidence of the value placed upon these objects at this time.

Sconces—wall-lights, became peculiarly domiciled in England, from those at Hampton Court with handsomely scrolled back-plates reflecting the candle-light, to those of cast bronze in Renaissance design, perhaps with the primitive attempt to include the Tudor rose in a Renaissance pattern (Fig. 75). Metal chandeliers were still imported and were more elaborate and intricate. Candle-beams of wood might be called chandeliers and have "latten candelstikkes." By the end of the Elizabethan period (1558–1603) wooden or hanging lights instead of rare luxuries were found in most houses. Lanterns were simple compared with Italian Renaissance models; a "lanthorne of white lattyn" might be placed on the stairs; one of "white tynne" plate against a wall; one of carved wood with glass; but ordinarily they were of horn. Lamps seemed to have developed little from the primitive type.

The 17th Century saw that excess of luxury and indulgence which brought the sharp protest of the Reformation (1649), only to swing back to greater indulgence in the Restoration (1660) of Charles II. The French taste of Louis XIV prevailed. Silver, plain or gilt, was used for elaborate lighting fixtures but latten was common, with pewter and wood, pottery and iron for humbler uses. *Champlevé* enamel was used on decorated brass candlesticks early in the Century. But everything that may be said of 17th Century lighting fixtures is said with one eye on silver, for silver was used with that magnificence we associate with precious metals and with a sumptuousness and largeness that astonishes us even to-day in the chandeliers, sconces, and candlesticks of the period.

A superb pair of candlesticks (Fig 70) is 43½ in. high, the base 17 in. and the top 12 in. in diameter. The stem is composed of various vase and urn forms so frankly designed we feel that we might dismount them element by element for separate uses. Above the base is a large urn of classic type, and above it rests a distinct high-shouldered vase, and above this another urn. These three recognizable motifs are nicely harmonized however and joined by shorter pedestal or basket-like sections. Still the whole outline smacks more of the ringed candlestick of northern predilection than of the unified creation of the Italian Renaissance, and is of peculiar interest for this reason. The ornament is handled with great skill from the rimming of the three feet—half-circular disks, to the edging of the wide *bobèche*. The gadrooning on the various members adds an element of distinction, a sort of precision if not severity which offsets the elaborate *repoussé* ornament in acanthus leafage and more natural forms. The base is rimmed on its rounded molding with a banding of alternate motifs composed of grouped acanthus ornament and natural fruits and flowers. It seems as if almost every type of ornament known to the silversmith had been incorporated, with the exception of animal and human forms and heraldic devices. These pieces reward careful study. Here is the

70. These superb silver candlesticks were made about 1685. They stand 43½ in. high and are magnificent examples of the design and workmanship of the period. Courtesy Crichton & Co.

formal classical gadrooning, beading, and decorative moldings; and a saucy almost Rococo flare to the pedestal of the high-shouldered vase placed just above the middle of the stem. So rich and varied is the ornament that the eye never tires of following it point by point. Far from fussiness, its majestic proportions give it great dignity.

Lavish *repoussé* and chasing in a veritable splurge of ornament disappeared when the Britannia standard for purer silver with less alloy was in force (1696–1720), for sharply cut ornament would not hold its form in polishing such soft silver.

Silver candlesticks were made in Medieval forms well into the 17th Century, but the wide grease pan descended gradually and disappeared while the nozzle became a distinct capital. The flatter

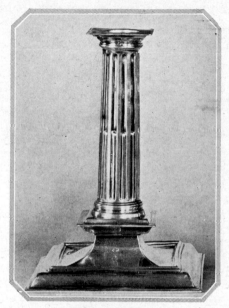

71. A column candlestick in silver with square dished foot. It bears the London hall-mark for 1682–3. Courtesy Victoria and Albert Museum.

circular foot was used, as well as the heavy oriental and Venetian type. 17th Century column candlesticks (Fig. 71) have a very modern look for we have long used this type especially in silver and pottery, and find them as acceptable to-day amid our universal possibility of choice as when they were the most fashionable model of the period. In the evolution of the candlestick there now appeared the classic fluted column and the baluster stem as well as the older trumpet-shaped foot. The usual type incorporated various vase and urn forms as in the Renaissance. Foliage ornament gave way to natural flowers often of disproportionate size; though the acanthus was still used. One example (Fig. 72) decorated with these tremendous flowers has deer leaping among them. The animals are extremely minute compared with the size of the flowers, which adds a curious though unnatural interest.

72. The silver-gilt original of this candlestick was made in 1663–4. Note the grease pan high on the cylindrical stem and the flowers of disproportionate size in the elaborate *repoussé* ornament. Courtesy Victoria and Albert Museum.

A factor common to many of the candlesticks of this period is the very large grease pan set almost half way up on the candle stem. Imported bronze candlesticks were fashionable. Snuffers came into use. Latten and pewter candlesticks followed silver designs but more simply turned, with trumpet base and wide grease pan at varying heights on the stem. Ringed pewter and brass candlesticks (Fig. 73) were common. Brass and wood, especially walnut, were combined and later elaborated. Enameled brass candlesticks were still made with Medieval monsters, human figures, and floral ornament. Pottery followed prevailing types, occasionally with picturesque additions (Fig. 74). Candlesticks of blown glass and of molded glass appeared in the late Century and evolved shapes similar to the stems of drinking glasses of the period. Candelabra were similar in design to candlesticks, occasionally made with removable branches.

73. Typical examples of the wide grease pan in these brass candlesticks. The pair is ringed in the 17th Century manner. Courtesy Victoria and Albert Museum.

74. This earthenware candlestick dated 1649 has the picturesque addition of many handles. Courtesy Victoria and Albert Museum.

Brass backplates to increase the light were followed by mirrors. Silver sconces, many for a single candle, were elaborately designed with chasing and *repoussé* work: acanthus, husk, festoon, shell, basket of fruit, flowers, oak, acorn, cupid, ribbon, scroll, and crest. The candle branch might be a man's arm or a simple S-shaped scroll of glass or metal. An Elizabethan sconce of cast bronze (Fig. 75) is typical of the ornamental enrichment of the period. Its

75. A charming Elizabethan sconce of cast bronze proves that Elizabethan rooms were not devoid of beauty. Courtesy Bagués, Inc.

backplate is elaborately shaped. The design is that of a pavilion upheld by double columns and topped by a draped canopy. A woman's bust is placed within, on a pedestal, below which falls a tasseled lambrequin. Above her head is a rayed motif like a sunburst. Above the canopy there is a classic urn with fine scrollwork on either side. The backplate is much broader at the bottom and outlined by rich scrolls terminating in a shell motif, which grew in popularity during the following periods. The bracket for a single candle is shaped in a rounded S-curve and bears a well proportioned *bobèche* and a neat ringed candle socket.

Chandeliers for candles, often called "branches," were of silver, rock-crystal, glass, and wood; imported ones of glass and brass. Silver branched chandeliers set the mode with ornate acanthus, gadrooning, and cupids, many with escutcheons for the palaces. Brass chandeliers with huge solid balls on their baluster stems,

76. England used many of these brass chandeliers imported from the Netherlands in the 17th Century. Courtesy French & Co.

and their scrolled candle branches in one, two, or three tiers were highly decorative.

The treatment of the baluster stems as well as the branches varies widely in these brass chandeliers. In one example (Fig. 76) the large ball hangs well below the branches, ending in an elongated finial and ring. Above this ball the stem is turned in vase and ringed motifs with some accent given to the rings. The lower tier of branches is set about midway on the stem, and they sweep quite low in a reversed or S-scroll. The candle sockets are very much elongated goblet motifs set on neat saucer-like grease pans. The upper tier is placed at the top of the stem, and these branches curve down even more closely bringing the candle sockets into a smaller circle than those of the lower tier. The sockets on this upper tier are deep and tubular. A ring much larger than that at the lower end is fitted into the stem from which the chandelier is hung. The characteristic tendency to sharpen the outlines of the turned rings, found on furniture legs especially in Italy and Spain, is occasionally seen in the baluster stems of these chandeliers. On some of them the rings are emphasized rather unpleasantly. An example (Fig. 77) in which the rings are well spaced and inconspicuous, has a single tier of branches; the position of the upper tier being occupied by small reflectors set out on scrolled branches. These reflectors are shaped like shallow bowls or saucers, and above them are smaller shaped reflectors elaborated with piercing. The candle branches do not curve out directly from the stem but start with a formal rustic branch work. Alternating between the branches are the same circular reflectors as above and small doves which add a sprightly ornament. The urn sockets and *bobèches* are well formed and in no way exaggerated. The ring motifs are nicely used, appearing even on the big lower ball.

Less abrupt outlines also characterize some of these baluster stems. One (Fig. 78) incorporates a well shaped vase motif with several knops. The candle branches are of conventionalized rustic scrolling, the *bobèches* quite wide and the urn sockets slightly elongated. The baluster is topped by a small figure of the Virgin set in an open oval framework. Some of these brass chandeliers are trim little things with a single tier of candle branches, each with a little ornamental scrollwork to set it off; some merely rustic, others are distinctly the acanthus leafage though not elaborate. One type made in bronze or brass has the large ball placed on top of the short stem, and the candle branches just below it. Another imposing piece is topped by a figure. Its branches are in two

77. Reflectors were occasionally used to increase the light from these 17th Century brass chandeliers which had a great vogue. Courtesy French & Co.

tiers. The ball is enormous and the finial—an inverted vase, large in proportion. Other members of the stem are jar or ring-turned. The branches of both tiers depend in low sweeping reversed curves, the lower ones ornamented with griffins near the stem. The candle sockets show a decided variant from the ordinary Flemish type, preserving the urn form but very tall and slender, and highly sophisticated with extremely wide *bobèche*. Such variants are frequently found in the Flemish and German chandeliers. Those

78. A delightful variant of the scrolled candle branches is shown in this 17th Century brass chandelier with a baluster stem. Courtesy French & Co.

of central Europe, especially Russian, Polish, or Hungarian, are often ornamented with an eagle.

Imported rock-crystal was cut in England to ornament elaborate chandeliers with festoons and pendants like those at Hampton Court. Glass chandeliers with cut pendants followed imported Dutch models with big balls like the brass chandeliers. Some were made without pendants. In the late 17th Century chandeliers of wood elaborately carved and gilded were in vogue. They were more massive and had fewer branches than the metal chandeliers, their stems formed of bulbous or polygonal motifs and the branches magnificently carved in the typical 17th Century handling of the acanthus. Early examples show French influence.

There was little interest in French inventions for lamps. Glass was more generally used in lanterns; one about 1600, octagon shaped, has leaded green bottle glass. Pierced drums were used for night lights, but candle-light was supreme.

CHAPTER IX

ENGLISH—18TH CENTURY

THE embarrassment of riches in 18th Century English lighting fixtures offers a problem almost as great as the lack of earlier examples. Candle-light was still supreme and England was still satisfied with it, although a place was made for an oil lamp in many a fine home. The steady flame of the wick fed with oil, if a trifle less delightful than the flicker of candle-light, made reading more practical, and when the Adam Brothers deigned to design a lamp, their unquestioned authority made such things acceptable.

But much happened in the 18th Century before the advent of the classic revival sponsored by the Adam Brothers; and the sequence of the period styles is distinctly marked, however brief their sway. Early in the century the Dutch style still held with William-and-Mary (1689–1702); its simplification in the Queen Anne period (1702–1714) was followed by the Georgian in which French influence, which had always more or less swayed English taste, was predominant under George II (1727–1760). The other nations, especially oriental, contributed their quota, and out of it all the styles of Chippendale, Heppelwhite, and Sheraton stand for specific accomplishments.

Students of the period styles trace their beginning, their florescence, and decline with some exactitude in furniture, silver, and other things, but the dates noted here merely indicate the reigns of the sovereigns whose names have attached to the styles. It is a bit helpful to remember the sequence of Baroque, Rococo, and Neo-classic, so marked in French, Italian, and Spanish work, for the century opened with the influence of the French Baroque of Louis XIV, vital in earlier Jacobean days; and the Flemish variants, and the Dutch slant only ushered in the Rococo of the Georgian period, which gave way to the new classic vogue. We shall leave the classic revival for another chapter, tracing the other styles well into the reign of George III (1760–1820), for they ran concurrently with the classic revival for some time.

The kinds of fixtures remained the same as in the 17th Century, with perhaps greater emphasis on the decorative wall-lights, which were apt to be conspicuous, and a more general use of the chandelier. With the opening up of the world to wide-spread commerce came foreign wares and arts, and a more sophisticated variety of things quickly reflected in the variety of designs for fixtures. Materials, too, played their part: porcelain, pottery, and glass grew yearly more plentiful. Chelsea porcelain ornaments with candle sockets, were however more ornamental than useful (Fig. IX). Waterford glass candelabra and girandoles became moderate priced luxuries, which to day are as nectar and ambrosia to collectors. To these add brass, plain or hung with glass pendants; iron, often colored and partly gilded; carved wood; and silver.

Many silversmiths made nothing but candlesticks and gained a fame for them. Candlesticks were legion and fancy played riot with their forms, especially in the mid-Century. Silver yielded more conservatively to whim, and the orderly evolution of the baluster candlestick with all its dignity and beauty gives to 18th Century table candlesticks and candelabra an eminence justly deserved. Then, too, in the days of Rococo with its fanciful dissymmetrical outlines and its whimsical use of scroll and rockery, Lamerie, the great silversmith, was at work and set a standard many tried to reach. So that to boast a set of four table candlesticks with a candelabrum made by an 18th Century silversmith is something to start a dinner finely even to this day.

While the Britannia standard was in force (1696–1720), silver designs were simple. Silver appeared chiefly in hand and table candlesticks, smaller shapes to hold tapers on the writing table, and in candelabra; more rarely in sconces with or without mirrors. Candelabra were designed with baluster stems and scrolled branches, often made in sets with two or four candlesticks to match. So admirably was the design suited to the object that silver plate made later than George II has little good to show, in the opinion of collectors, except reproductions. The Revocation of the Edict of Nantes brought highly trained French craftsmen to England, which largely accounts for the beauty and perfection of 18th Century lighting fixtures as of all other industrial art objects.

The 18th Century opened with the William-and-Mary type of silver candlestick having a polygonal stem and base. Stems were also of simple baluster type on a square base, with the corners cut off, set back, and rounded. Queen Anne types were still plain surfaced but their outlines were delicate, not clumsy. Octagonal stems were frequent, depending for effectiveness upon their faceting in lieu of ornament. The base was square with corners cut off or set back and rounded. The Huguenot silversmiths then domiciled in England, accustomed as they were to elaborate French work, enlivened their candlesticks with grease pans that were convex and gadrooned.

Silver candlesticks during the reign of George I had baluster stems. They were frequently octagonal and faceted on a molded octagonal base. One pair (Fig. 79) made by David Green of Foster Lane with the London hall-mark for the year 1718–19, is but six inches high. Many taper-sticks were made in this type and scarcely lower. The Britannia standard held until the middle of the reign of George I, so that many George I candlesticks were of this plain baluster type. Paul Lamerie, the Frenchman, whom his admirers rank as the greatest silversmith since Benvenuto Cellini, was at work in England at this time and made some of these plain virile candlesticks, although he later became famous for his beautiful handling of Rococo design. A set of four candlesticks made by him in 1718 is of this early type. The law regulating the purity of the metal had a radical effect upon the work of the silversmiths, which had not been so lacking in ornament since the days of the Puritans. It was the dominant factor in the candlesticks and candelabra made in the reign of William-and-Mary, Queen Anne, and the early years of George I. All collectors of English silverware have the words "Britannia standard" on the tip of the tongue, and constantly seek with great rivalry the pieces made in this period. Delicate engraved ornament disap-

peared, and only faceting or deeply sunk gadrooning and fluting
were typical of these pieces. As soon as Parliament restored the
old silver standard regulating the alloy, candlesticks were made
more massive and heavier. These heavier plain pieces, as well as
the Rococo forms then coming into fashion, were not hammered
out of the metal as previously, but were cast in a mold. The rough

79. A pair of hexagonal silver candlesticks made by David Green with the London hall-mark for 1718-9. Courtesy Victoria and Albert Museum.

unfinished surface underneath makes this evident. Undecorated
candlesticks continued to be made after the law had been revoked
but were not typical of the period. *Régence* design had some influence upon their ornament but the Rococo soon became popular.
The Rococo vogue lasted about forty years, starting near the end
of the reign of George I in 1725, covering the whole of the reign
of George II (1727–60) and five years of the reign of George III
until 1765. But in the last years of this period it remained as mere
ornament and not structure. Fashion had grown weary of the
irregularity of the Rococo outline about the year 1757.

Diagonal gadrooning, popular in the Louis XV period in France,
was well liked in England and was much used on baluster candle-

sticks. The Huguenot silversmiths and their followers handled Louis XV design with that native *esprit* peculiarly French. Lamerie became so completely master of this style that he could make a thing of joy out of a mere candle-holder. The French vogue was then in full swing, stems were still baluster, octagonal or hexagonal, and often had that high-shouldered look peculiar to the style. There was a free use of rich ornament and much swirling and oblique gadrooning. Human half figures sometimes formed the stem as in France, resting on solid bases and supporting foliated nozzles. Bases were elaborately shaped and scalloped, and decorated with conventional shell motifs. The nozzles were also elaborately scalloped and occasionally were removable. Flowers were added to the characteristic ornament of shell and scrollwork, and these were wrought naturalistically. When the Chinese vogue made its appearance in English furnishings, it was not lacking in silver candlesticks. A pair by John Cafe made in 1751–2 incorporates the seated figure of a Chinese as part of the stem. It will be recalled that the hall-marks were placed underneath the early pieces, but in the reign of George III the marks were placed on the outside edge of the bases, except when a piece was cast, then it was marked inside.

A process of plating silverware was developed at Sheffield about 1750, the finished work being known as Sheffield Plate. Layers of silver and copper were fused together, rolled into sheets, and then made into candlesticks with all the embossing and chasing fashionable in solid silver. The process was continued until about 1840 at Sheffield, and elsewhere until the cheaper electroplating was introduced. Sheffield Plate candlesticks and candelabra rarely followed simple models but imitated the Rococo ornament of Chippendale, and are especially suitable with Chippendale furniture. Later examples showed a decided classic influence.

Brass candlesticks followed silver designs, the grease pan octagonal or round, convex with gadrooning. Kitchen candlesticks retained the earlier knopped stem. Pewter was for humbler uses in simple forms. Rushlight holders were still of iron for kitchen and cottage, often made with substantial wooden bases and adjustable ratchets. Candle sockets and pincers for the rushlights were often combined in the same fixture and this was frequently suspended; one example having two branches like a simple chandelier. The smiths embellished them a bit too with a tiny cock, a fleur-de-lis, a fancy twist or curled end. Wood was not confined to the cottage but artistically handled with ingenious turning and carving. A walnut base might support a simple tubular brass candlestick. Some early examples were rather small with plain baluster stem on a circular foot and an outer socket to hold a tall glass wind-shield extending high above the candle flame, especially for use in hallways. Chippendale and others made many varieties of wooden candlesticks, particularly of mahogany, beautifully turned and carved with acanthus and gadrooning. Classic urns with brass sockets often topped their tall, exceedingly graceful baluster stems.

Ornamental porcelain candlesticks were made of Chelsea (Fig. IX), Bow, Derby, and other wares, especially with human figures in rustic settings realistically colored. Candlesticks of Battersea enamel were highly ornate in the French taste of the period; but glass candlesticks were unique in their development. Whether blown or molded their designs followed the fashion of the stemmed drinking glass of the day—early baluster, later with vase forms. Early candlesticks of clear Waterford glass with its darkish hue hinting of blue, green, and black are greatly prized to-day.

Taper sticks or holders followed candlestick designs in silver and brass and were indispensable on the writing desk for heating scaling wax. A silver taper stick of the Queen Anne period is extremely interesting as it harks back to earlier forms in its broad low rounded base with a wide grease pan set high up on the stem. This grease pan however is but a memory of earlier models, for it is impractical with its open piercing and is purely ornamental. The stem of this little taper holder, which measures just under five inches, is a curious combination of motifs: between the base and the grease pan it is a truncated cone upon which sets a baluster stem, the top motif of which is a familiar vase set upside down. Above this, occupying nearly one-third of the stem, is the long, ringed, tubular nozzle, nicely molded at top. The broad base is pierced with a wide banding containing the inscription: "Queen Anne 1702."

The candelabrum standard followed the style of candlesticks, with polygonal and faceted foot, the branches quite plain, later

80. A superb George II candelabrum made by Paul Crespin about 1730, formerly owned by the Duke of Marlborough. Courtesy Crichton & Co.

ornamented, and occasionally removable. A superlative example (Fig. 80) made about 1730, shows the handling of this queen of metals at its best. Though made at the time when the Rococo had already appeared it is symmetrical in outline, with classic ornament somewhat freely interpreted. The stem is a complete candlestick of baluster type with a hexagonal shaft, the facets engraved in a formal design. The foot is round, with four conventional ornaments applied on its well shaped moldings. At the top of the

shaft are placed three finely executed busts. Above the shaft a
well shaped member supports an elaborate interpretation of the
classic urn. Into this urn are set the three scrolled candle branches,
which are braced by semicircular scrolls, and proceed out of the
mouths of animal masks. They terminate in in-curved scrollings
decorated with applied ornaments and pendent garlands. The

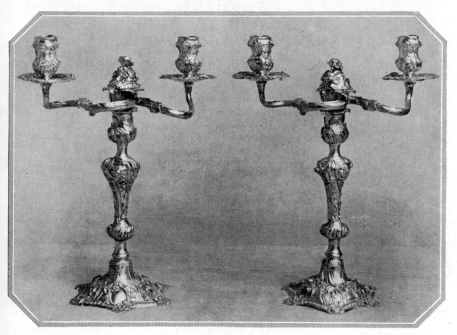

81. Candelabra made at the end of the reign of George II by John Hyatt and
Chas. Semore, in 1759. Courtesy Crichton & Co.

bobèches are saucer-like with scrolled outlines, and the sockets
are a different rendering of the classic urn from that on the standard. This candelabrum, which is 32 in. high, was formerly at
Blenheim Palace.

A pair of three-light candelabra (Fig. 81) made by John Hyatt
and Chas. Semore of London, in 1759 at the end of the reign of
George II, illustrates admirably the English use of the Rococo
style. They are 15¼ in. high; the width of the candle branches

being 12 in. The stem is a complete candlestick, its urn-shaped socket ornamented with swirling leafage. Its vase motif is high-shouldered in the Louis XV style, decorated with formal scrolling, and naturalistic leaf scrolls and flowers. The knop below is formed of swirling petals; the plain incurving stem and ring offsetting it admirably. The base shapes charmingly into its molded edge and is ornamented by formal scrolls and lovely natural roses and foliage. The two candle arms swirl outward, partially encircling the stem in Rococo fashion, and are themselves delicately embellished by leafage. The flat *bobèches* and urn-shaped sockets have their forms swathed in scroll and foliage ornament. A finial of natural flowers is placed in the third candle socket so that the candelabrum can be used for two as well as three candles. This is a superb example of the Rococo style without riot or exaggeration.

Girandoles were often of wood, carved and gilded, and were a highly decorative feature of 18th Century rooms. This was the Golden Age of English wood-workers and their brackets and sconces were splendid. Whether carved by Grinling Gibbons in the French style of the *Régence* or the fantastic creations later in vogue, they were indispensable elements of the 18th Century interior. An example by this famous wood-carver (Fig. 82) made about 1700 is of mahogany, 16 in. high for two lights. Its back-plate is an oval upright topped by a convex shell, flanked by twin fish. The base is a cut capital formed of various moldings, one a formalized petaled blossom. This pedestal supports a tall upright shell down the concave bowl of which descends a dolphin with a crystal ball in its mouth. Two finely curved brackets are fitted into the lower curving of the shell. They spring from acanthus clusters, broaden greatly, and end in superb acanthus *bobèches* with depending instead of upturned leaves. The candle cups are short and molded, with a beaded banding. Turn the illustration upside down and the *bobèche* and socket show a more familiar form.

Early examples of girandoles in wood, carved and partly gilded, were in the form of a vase with a flaming finial and scrolled candle branches. Placed on a corbel wall bracket, carved in the scroll and acanthus ornament of the period, they were extremely decorative. William Kent, the architect, and other artists of the 18th Century, designed many ornamental wall brackets for candelabra, vases, busts, and other ornaments. Girandoles in the later style of Chippendale, of which there are many examples in *The*

82. A superb sconce made by Grinling Gibbons in mahogany about 1700. The dolphin holds a crystal ball in its mouth. Courtesy American Art Association.

Gentleman and Cabinet-Maker's Director, carry an ever-increasing number of candle branches.

Wall-lights became more and more popular as long as candles were in use. Beginning with the sconces of William-and-Mary type in silver or brass there came a freer use of different materials in the later Century. The backplates followed the period styles. They had elaborate scrolled outlines and the whole plate was covered with ornament in the William-and-Mary period. The outline might be scalloped and gadrooned, dish-shaped, or elaborately scrolled and shield-shaped; ornamented with acanthus, cupids, festoons, gadrooning, etc. Brass was the common material; silver for luxury, with splendid *repoussé* ornament. The eight silver sconces in the State Bedroom of William III in Hampton Court are notable examples.

A fine pair in silver made by John Rand of London in the reign of William-and-Mary, 1703, and accurately reproduced (Fig. 83), shows the sort of elaboration that was possible in the softer metal during the period of the Britannia standard. It is worked

83. One of a pair of William-and-Mary silver sconces, reproduced from those made by John Rand of London, in 1703. Courtesy Crichton & Co.

boldly without the fineness possible in harder metal like that of the silver sconce made in 1790 (Fig. 85). In this earlier example, the gadrooning, beading, figure, and floral motifs are all full-bodied, more effective in a wall-plate than a candlestick. Cupids support the broad flaming finial and hold sprays of fruit and flowers in their opposite hands. They are seated on the scrolled sides of the center shield. Below them are two eagles' heads from whose beaks hang floral and fruit garlands which curve around the base with its acanthus and grape finial. The frank surface use of the hall-marks is clearly seen on the scale ornament to the right. Two ringed candle arms support rather flat beaded *bobèches* with urn-shaped sockets.

Simple in form and outline under Queen Anne (Fig. 84), the typical shape whether of metal or mirror was long and quite narrow, often spreading a little at the top. The mirror back was popular, sometimes cut in a simple ornamental design, often a conventional shell motif. From the beginning of the Century,

84. This Queen Ann mirror backed sconce with pewter bracket has the incised shell ornament characteristic of the period. Courtesy French & Co.

plain or ornamental S-shaped scrolls, especially of brass, were used for candle brackets with inconspicuous backplates. One or two small candle branches set near the plate were ordinarily used with large or elaborate backplates. Mirrors were increasingly fashionable for backplates in the Georgian period, but splendidly carved and gilded wood was not abandoned. The convex mirror in a circular gilt frame surmounted by an eagle was used at this time and became popular in America. With the introduction of Rococo ornament about 1725, some exquisite silver sconces were made, the early work being restrained, often incorporating a coat-of-arms. Sconces of later date were apt to be fantastic, often showing Chinese influence.

A restrained example (Fig. 85) is well illustrated in the silver sconce made at Sheffield in 1790 during the reign of George III. The name Sheffield has been so widely associated with the plated ware known as Sheffield Plate that it is often confused with Sheffield silver. This sconce is of silver, its backplate incorporating the royal coat-of-arms. The fine handling of acanthus ornament by these Sheffield silversmiths is one of their special accomplish-

85. This silver mirror backed sconce, 1790, is typically ornamented with the royal coat-of-arms and excellent acanthus scrolling. Courtesy French & Co.

ments and is notable in this piece. We have among the silverware our thoughtful ancestors provided for us a set of four silver coasters made at Sheffield with the most superb handling of acanthus ornament. In fact they are the handsomest coasters we have ever seen and bear little but acanthus ornament. They belonged to Archibald S. Bulloch, son of the first President, as he was then called, of Georgia, our maternal ancestor as he was of Theodore Roosevelt. Attention is especially called to the modeling of the acanthus in these silver coasters because of the beauty which this motif often achieved in Sheffield work. The whole design is very satisfying and comes nearer to the dear familiar things to which we have been long accustomed in everyday living, than the cruder ornament of earlier days.

Chandeliers were still called "branches" as in the 17th Century but gradually became known as chandeliers; those of glass, keeping the French name of *lustre,* were imported until the mid-Century. The highly decorative carved wooden chandeliers, gilded or painted and parcel-gilt, retained their prominence, while the *lustre* became more generally used. Chandeliers were made of silver in the Louis XIV style but were not common. They were made of silver with two tiers of branches hung with rock-crystal. When of ivory they were small and compact but very rare. If of brass in various designs they were often reminiscent of Flemish and Dutch models with big balls on the stems. They were also made of copper gilt; of wrought-iron sometimes decorated with color and gilding; and of brass elaborately hung with rock-crystal. Imported *lustres* either showed the metal frame or were all of glass, elaborately or simply cut.

Brass chandeliers were occasionally of more elaborate design than the simple knobbed and ball stem. One model (Fig. 86) which inspired American craftsmen who repeated these balusters in carved wood, has a stem which reflects in simplified form the superb gilded carved wooden chandeliers of the period. It is an early 18th Century example, formerly in St. Mary's Church, Newmarket. The baluster hints of the jar form of the Italian sanctuary lamp, but barely hints, in its large bulb from which spring the reversed curves of the ringed candle branches, ornamented by occasional leaf tips. There is deep gadrooning on its top canopy-like member as on the lower member which ends with a conventional finial. The *bobèches* are broad and deep, and the candle sockets hint distantly of the classic urn.

The wooden chandeliers with one, two, or three tiers of candle branches were splendidly carved with gadrooning, reeding, and acanthus, French designs with canopy or lambrequin and tassels being favorites. William Kent designed many of these chandeliers for his clients. Baroque models were followed by the Rococo, and many whimsical motifs were incorporated in both styles: palms, umbrellas, canopies of leaves, eagles, satyrs' masks, laurel, wreaths, husks, etc. The carving was sometimes inspired by the silver plate

designs of the period. The finials ending the stems were delight-
fully conceived, occasionally of fruit and flowers. The carving
was vigorous and highly ornate, with floral and foliage motifs in
the florid taste of the mid-Century.

Glass chandeliers and girandoles were charmingly designed,
the metal framework sometimes entirely covered with glass tubing.

86. A brass chandelier of the early 18th Century with finely scrolled candle
branches. Its short bulbous stem was copied in wood in America. Courtesy Victoria and Albert Museum.

The stem often incorporated a large glass ball, was topped with a
canopy and was hung with pendants at top and bottom. The
curved branches might have elaborated scrolling and loops, each
topped by a spire; or the whole baluster was quite simply formed
of cut glass members with twisted branches springing from a
large bowl. Glass *lustres* were much in vogue and in the mid-
Century ladies amused themselves by redraping them according to
the changing fashions. Rock-crystal chandeliers might be elaborately festooned on a metal frame surmounted by a crown, the

whole design delicate and graceful; or heavy looking, no metal apparent, with the festoons and crown studded to give a jewel effect.

Eighteenth Century England was too well satisfied with candlelight reflected on the polished mahogany of its comfortable furniture to give much heed to the lamps the French were inventing. Still Argand lamps were found in many homes by the end of the Century. Great numbers of candles were burned and craftsmen used much ingenuity in locating holders better to distribute their light around the room. Candle sockets were fitted, often somewhat insecurely, to various pieces of furniture in the mid-Century. Designers of the Chippendale school made their candle branches more ornamental to harmonize with the objects to which they were attached, decorating them in the Rococo motifs of the period. Sheraton's use of candle brackets on his small dressing mirrors and his designs for tripod candle stands were the acme of elegance. 18th Century candle stands are charming little furnishing accessories and follow the period styles in furniture. Elaborate stands for candelabra like the French *torchères* were often highly ornate with gesso ornament in the reign of George I. Candle stands were not always of table height; some were tiny contrivances to place on a table and had a mechanical screw device for raising and lowering the top on which the candlestick was placed. Particularly interesting are those stands whose tops were shaped to fit accurately the whimsical outlines of the silver candlesticks whose Rococo designs were often the extreme of elaboration.

Lanterns became an architectural accessory especially designed for use in entrance halls and passages, the ornament following the successive period styles. For convenience they were frequently placed against the wall or hung from wall brackets. Some examples of the early 18th Century have two brackets, one to support the globelike glass holding the light, the upper bracket for the flaring glass protecting shade hung above it.

Hanging lanterns had frames of metal or wood, iron, copper, bronze, brass; walnut or mahogany, the wood handsomely carved in acanthus scrolling and gilded. They were oval, hexagonal, or octagonal, often topped with a crown. When following French models they were frequently quite beautiful.

At last the English lantern came into its own, a century or two after those of Italy, Spain, and France. A fine example (Fig. 87), made about 1760–70 is of gilded bronze to hang in a Georgian hall. The framing is of plain strap-work, the top latticed, and the whole

87. A Georgian lantern, 1760–70, of gilded bronze with beautiful convex glass panes and cut glass bowl and ball ending in a metal berry finial. Courtesy French & Co.

structure except the lattice completely covered with acanthus leafage. Long leaves outline the oval panes; short curling ones compose the crown; rosettes of acanthus tip the cut glass bowl forming the bottom of the lantern, and finish the pendent cut glass ball from which drops a metal berry finial. One of the convex panels opens with a key to light the candle.

Nothing could be more effective than the wall fixture, resembling a *demi-lanterne*, designed to protect the candle with its candlestick which stood on a bracket, the bracket surrounded

with a glassed cabinet open at top, framed in a delectable un-
dulating cornice of carved mahogany. Sometimes a touch of
chinoiserie is seen in a rectangular portable lantern with fretwork
and pagoda top. Such a lantern might be hung on the wall as
well as placed on a small table to light a side stairway or a wind-
ing passage. Chippendale had many lantern designs in his gayest
modes.

CHAPTER X

ADAM—AND 19TH CENTURY

THE beauty of classic design again stirred English artists and craftsmen in the 18th Century as it had in the 16th, when "the tight little isle" felt the influence of the Italian Renaissance during the reign of Henry VIII. Both revivals were inspired by the unearthing of beautiful antiques; the earlier by the digging up of classic sculpture on the Roman hills, the later by the excavating done at the cities of Pompeii and Herculaneum.

The modern world is so accustomed to archæological discovery that it is difficult for us to realize the stir which the excavation of these long-buried cities caused in Europe and America. France, with her native sensitiveness to beauty, quickly felt the effects in her furnishings; and those successful English architects, the Adam Brothers, carried classic composition and ornament into great favor in the last half of the 18th Century. Fashionable England turned quickly to the new order of things but English conservatism yielded slowly. While an Adam drawing-room was the acme of fashionable elegance, the style of Chippendale and his school suited Britain too well to be completely abandoned for the classic, so that these styles ran concurrently.

Lighting fixtures with the Adam Brothers became an integral part of the decorative scheme, which in its turn was integral with the architectural features of the room, as it was in France at this time; and English interior decoration as an art came by gradual stages into being.

Silver was principally used for candlesticks and candelabra; bronze more sparingly for chandeliers and lamps; iron almost abandoned; brass and *ormolu* often used with other materials; pewter and zinc where silver-plated ware was too expensive; wood was carved and gilded, principally for wall brackets; enamel remained in vogue. There was a new interest in marble, prized in classic art, especially in the various mottled and colored stones like Derbyshire spar. Porcelain held its own, not only for ornamental candlesticks, but as accessories in the composition of elaborate fixtures, especially classic vases and urns. Pottery reached its zenith in Wedgwood's jasper ware in which minute effects, as delicate as carved cameos, were obtained in white on a colored ground. But on the whole porcelain and pottery did not yield naturally to classic forms. Glass was paramount. It was widely used for festoons and pendants to decorate chandeliers, sconces, girandoles, candelabra, and even the more simple single candlesticks.

About 1760 there was a decided change in the evolution of the silver candlestick. The fluted column, fashionable in the 17th Century, reappeared but with a Corinthian capital instead of a simple molded nozzle. The concave molded foot was not immediately discarded, but the high spreading foot was general. Earlier forms were gradually abandoned. Besides the fashionable Corinthian column, there was a model with a square base, typically ornamented with rams' heads and festoons, the stem expanding above it to the circular or vase-shaped socket. The column was elongated in a George III model and bore a nozzle or socket pan. Josiah Wedgwood's classic designs were worked in silver during the later 18th Century; the socket was the classic urn, and the decoration somewhat ornate with festoons, flowers, and masks. After about 1780 the stems of silver candlesticks, when not columnar, took the form of a pedestal either rectangular or cylindrical, tapering downward; the foot concave or round. The classic urn socket was retained and the decorations were husks, pendants, pateræ, fluting, etc.

A pair 12 in. high made in 1775 (Fig. 88) is typical. The square tapering stem, which acts as a base for the urn, was a welcome change from the baluster. All the details of these candlesticks bespeak the architect. The moldings are structurally considered and placed; their beading and fine leaf ornament inspired by classic motifs. The wreathed goat's head with garlands at the top of the panel or facet, carries thought back to the ancient classic worship of Bacchus. The nozzle reverts to the classic urn for inspiration, adding swags and other details for good measure. A more simple pair of the same type made by John Parsons & Co. with the Sheffield hall-mark for 1791–2, has delicate die-stamped ornament; light swags on the simply shaped urns and just below them on the pedestal; each face of which is bordered on the sides with

88. This silver candlestick with the typical Adam tapering rectangular stem was made in 1775. Courtesy The Anderson Galleries.

beading; the middle of the panel rounding at top into tablet form.

A Sheffield Plate candlestick made about 1780 is 11¼ in. high. The stem is a round column entwined diagonally with a festoon of a single strand of bell-flowers. The capital suggests the Corinthian but not very closely. The molding is squared and beaded on top, so that the capital acts as a candle nozzle. The base is square and slopes away from the column's square pedestal in a deep concave curve decorated with rams' heads at the corners. Drapery swags are caught in their mouths, one end hanging pendent and the other two ends parting to form a continuous drapery over the medallions in the center of the sides. Sheffield Plate and brass followed silver designs. Some late Sheffield Plate candlesticks were oval instead of circular and occasionally the urn was set directly on a short pedestal for a low candlestick. As in France,

Egyptian decoration had a certain vogue. A Sheffield Plate candle-stick made about 1770 has a stem of papyrus reeds with a capital of palms. The adjustable telescopic tube was sometimes used.

Besides brass and pewter, a sort of zinc known as tutenag was used for ordinary candlesticks. These were cast in classic shapes and ornamented with engraving. After the discovery of electro-plating, they were sometimes plated in silver. Glass candlesticks were plentiful. Late in the Century their stems were vase-shaped, tapered, or cylindrical. Clear glass was varied by enclosing opaque twists of air in the stem or small bubbles—"tears," in the glass. Stems were later ornamented with faceted cutting. By 1760 there was a great variety of shapes. Glass festoons and pendants were much used for candlesticks, candelabra, girandoles, wall-lights, and chandeliers. Pendant-hung candlesticks, candelabra, and gir-andoles were the fashionable mantel ornaments of the day. The cutting of the glass followed the same fashion as in the chande-liers; tall spires were typical.

Candlesticks of Battersea enamel were made with fluted bal-uster stems after 1770. Various colored and veined stones like Derbyshire spar were fashioned into candlesticks; a fine pair made about 1780 has an octagonal pillar, urn-shaped socket, and molded, circular domed foot on a square base. Wedgwood, the famous potter, revolutionized English household ornaments, which were previously crude. He made many candlesticks in his different wares. His black basaltes, ornaments of bacchantes and dolphins, chimeras and tritons, incorporated candlesticks in cornucopia form. His fine jasper ware in all colors, used as pedestals, medal-lions, etc., added to the variety of candle-holders offered the 18th Century homemaker.

Candelabra of silver or plated silver for the dining-table were of the same designs as candlesticks. The branches grew lighter and plainer to harmonize with the slender stems, but were often twisted in one or more loops. In the time of George III it was not uncommon to make a candlestick with one or more sets of branches, one for two lights, another for three, so that the lighting of a dinner-table could be increased conveniently. A simple hexagonal stem with restrained decoration was typical of the taste of the day. Hall-marks were still put on the outside of the candelabrum, except when it was cast; then they were marked inside. Sheffield Plate candelabra were similar to those in silver. An urn finial topped the stem, and branches were made for two or more lights.

Ornamental candelabra and girandoles were exceedingly popular. Flanking a clock on the mantelpiece they were more luxurious than single candlesticks however elaborately these might be hung with glass pendants and festoons. Glass candelabra had bases of metal, especially *ormolu*, china, or painted wood. Ornamental vases were incorporated in their designs as in France. Vases of "Blue John" or Derbyshire spar (fluor-spar) were mounted with pierced *ormolu* and bore candle branches which were sometimes removable. The covers of these vases were often reversible and, like the French *cassolettes*, held a socket for an extra candle. Ornamental classical vases with or without candle branches had an important place in the decorative schemes of the Adam Brothers. In the latter half of the 18th Century ornamental candelabra and girandoles were much used on pedestals, tables, and *guéridons*, especially designed for this purpose. An unusual tripod of iron designed by Robert Adam, about 1780, carries a small triangular top for a branched candelabrum with three candles. Its slender stem is vase-shaped, simply ornamented with water leaves. A *torchère* by him of carved and gilded wood, made about 1780, has serpents twisted downward around its stem, their heads lying outward along its base. The candelabrum surmounting it is a classic urn which is decorated appropriately with masks; the two candle branches carry four lights.

Adam's own designs for girandoles naturally are accepted as standards for the Adam style. They make use of classic vases with candle branches, or are designed with ancient Etruscan motifs. Girandoles in the Adam style were made of metal, occasionally of wood, and often of glass. One beautiful pair, with *ormolu* base set on feet, has a pedestal of jet. The tall glass spire upholds a small canopy from which hang pendants and festoons. The canopy is tipped by an urn-shaped finial exquisitely cut for brilliant effect. The candle branches are of glass somewhat fantastically twisted in loops. The *bobèches* of the calix-shaped candle sockets are hung with festoons and pendants of beautiful clear glass.

89. An exquisite Adam girandole with Wedgwood and metal base. Note the draped canopy and finial, tall spires and floral calix candle sockets. Courtesy French & Co.

Another pair (Fig. 89), four feet high, has the pedestal formed of Wedgwood jasper ware in cameo, white on blue, exquisitely mounted on an *ormolu* base; the upper arms bear two glass spires, and the whole framework is draped delicately with festoons and pendants of glass whose luster has the beautiful clear quality of rain drops.

In another girandole, 35 in. high by 22 wide, cut jet is used in the square tapering pedestal shaped much like the one of Wedgwood. Its quadrangular base of *ormolu* spreads more widely with cut corners and a deep incurved edge between them. The feet are ball shaped. This jet pedestal supports a domed *ormolu* member nicely ornamented, upon which rests a well proportioned cut glass ball. From this rises the spire commencing in a vase motif and ascending in a long tapering rectangular sword-like shaft, on the point of which is balanced the bowl-shaped canopy, much as some juggler would balance a plate on his sword point. Upon this canopy, somewhat broader than that in Fig. 89, is placed a covered ovoid urn, and from its edges hang strings of glass pendants. Long garlands are draped outward from it to the four candle branches. The stems of the piece are of cut glass, as are their *bobèches* and flower-like candle sockets which resemble those in Fig. 89. Garlands are draped between the brackets and strings of glass crystals hang from the *bobèches*. Longer strings depend from the large marguerites below the *bobèches* and end in large drops almost as lustrous as crystal.

Another girandole (Fig. VIII) of clear and amber Waterford glass combined is one of a set of six made about 1780. The metal base is of *ormolu*. The central shaft is surrounded by three broad scrolls set vertically to join the triangular molded base. They meet above and support the ball and vase members, which are of glass covered with a well-known cut pattern. The standard ascends well above the candle branches, but not to the extreme height which adds the element of special distinction to most of these girandoles or candelabra as they were quite generally called. This example of Waterford glass is more solid and substantial looking and less graceful than the one illustrated in Fig 89. The top is a faceted glass ball, below which hangs a large cut marguerite holding the three strings of crystals which are draped outward to the candle branches. These branches are of smooth glass with that texture characteristic of the Waterford works. The large *bobèches*

VIII. One of a set of six Waterford glass candelabra mounted in *ormolu*, combining clear and amber glass in the style of the period. Made about 1780. Height 34 in. Courtesy French & Co.

have turned-up scalloped edges, and the sockets have broad cups which flare well away from the candles. Other garlands and pendants drape the branches in the usual manner. It is a splendid substantial piece, 34 in. high and 22 in width, the amber glass adding greatly to its enrichment.

There was such an abundance of these candelabra that much ingenuity was employed to vary their designs, though all conformed more or less accurately to the accepted model of the day. Another fine pair with Waterford glass of finest quality and luster is 31 in. high. It is topped by an ornate eight-pointed star above its small canopy. The candle branches are cut, adding to the brilliancy of the piece, and further to enhance this brilliancy appears that attempt to simulate in glass the popular bow-knots of the day. This adds a curious irregularity to the design, but this motif is not uncommon. It appears in another pair of candelabra formed of plain uncut glass tubing made in smooth loops without any cutting. There is nothing more intriguing than these late 18th Century glass candelabra unless it is the wall brackets of similar design.

These were of course made without the pedestal. One distinguished sconce for four lights closely resembles Fig. 89, except that there are no spires. The ovoid vase on the stem is differently shaped and below it is another canopy, a trifle broader than that on top. From this depends a long finial beautifully cut in knops, and from the petaled edges of this flower-like canopy hang strings of crystals, each ending in a larger drop. The wall-plate for this sconce is an oval metal patera with a beaded edge. Other sconces resemble the more substantial and less ethereal looking Waterford candelabra. Another sconce of Waterford glass made between 1750–1800, is for three lights. The candle branches of plain tubing are placed in the mouth of a large vase. There is no canopy above and the strings of crystals depend from a large marguerite. The wall-plate is a highly ornamental oval with pierced design. Another Waterford sconce of the same period, possibly made at the end of the Century, lacks the long garlands and shows a certain sprightliness of design which has quite a modern look. The small bell-shaped canopy supports a large disk and is itself very lightly hung with four short strings of crystals. It is poised on the point of a very long spire which rests in a bowl, from which spring the two candle brackets, with a third scroll purely ornamental between them. This stands up vertically and holds the garlands well above the candle sockets but far below the canopy. A few very large drops add variety. The candle branches, sockets, and *bobèches* are all finely cut for added luster.

90. A wall bracket of carved and gilded wood, its stem decorated in classic ornament and upholding a jar of naturalistic flowers. Courtesy French & Co.

As in the Louis XVI interiors, those designed by the Adam Brothers incorporated such lighting fixtures as were considered requisite for the proper lighting of the room. Adam wall-lights add distinction and dignity to any interior in which they may be properly used. Adam's own designs are varied and ingenious, and wall-lights of this type were exceedingly popular and continued in favor until the advent of gas and electricity. Candle brackets ornamented the wall paneling or were placed beside the mirror of the over-mantel. One wall-light of this period, made of carved wood, is composed of a large half bowl from either side of which ringed candle branches curve gracefully downwards. Above this bowl-like motif are typical Adam vases and a classic tripod with mask and drapery. Carved and gilded wood was used for wall-lights resembling the French *appliques* of the Louis XVI period. A shaft composed of classic motifs (Fig. 90) might bear a large urn filled with

91. A typical Adam wall fixture with an oval mirror surrounded by delicate branches of leaves. Courtesy French & Co.

roses and fuchsias naturally carved; be draped with festoons; the candle branches curving low with splendidly modeled sockets. An oval mirror (Fig. 91) surrounded by a wreath and topped by a vase and flower motif, the whole design incorporated delicately in metal-work, is a typical Adam theme. It bears two curved candle branches. Ribbon bow-knots lent themselves appropriately to these *appliques* in which vase forms, festoons, griffins, water leaves, and delicate classic scrollwork combined to make charming fixtures.

But other wall brackets were not so lightly conceived. It must not be forgotten that the vogue for the eagle in decoration was a Georgian fashion as well as French and American. In England it started about 1790 and ran well into the Empire period until about 1810. A bracket of this time with a very long wall-plate fashioned like a torch is topped by a superb spread-eagle, with head turned backward toward his tail, and bearing in his mouth

92. The woman's figure in this wall bracket of carved and gilded wood is colored a dark brown. Courtesy French & Co.

a chain with four balls strung at intervals. The torch is bound with thongs and has a middle floral ornament and a scrolled leaf finial below. It is all made of wood carved and gilded except the two candle brackets which are of metal. They curve away from the backplate as if bound securely to it by crossed thongs. It is a virile piece, as are Figs. 90 and 92, very different from the delicacy of such conceptions as Fig. 93, or the fragility of many of the glass sconces. These however were not all fragile. Some were very solid looking, and useful in dignified interiors. Those of Waterford glass were often placed with good effect in the older wood paneled rooms of the Queen Anne as of the early Georgian period.

93. A bow-knot, griffins, and garland, ornament this somewhat unusual vase form which is treated in the typical Adam manner. Courtesy Frank Partridge, Inc.

The typical Adam chandelier was of glass, though wood and brass were still used. Rock-crystal was an extraordinary luxury. Glass chandeliers continued to be imported from France but those of English make became so popular they were shipped to the Continent on occasion. The working drawings for some of these chandeliers have been in possession of one English firm since 1780. The English chandeliers, like the French, were of several types. Some

were all glass; the earlier ones with plain glass tubing covering
the metal framework, the candle branches in S-shaped curves. In
later examples, made about 1788, the tubing was cut in gouges or
"hollows," adding to the brilliance of the refracted light. Some

94. This heavily cascaded chandelier made in the late 18th Century, has two
tiers of lights, one attached to the stem, the other springing from a corona.
Courtesy French & Co.

chandeliers were very delicately constructed and lightly and
sparsely garlanded; others were almost solidly cascaded with festoons, the coronas increasing in size and forming a large bowl-
like bottom (Fig. 94), draped with long pendants like fringe.
Interesting variations appeared in the designs for these chande-

liers. Some retained the center baluster stem composed of different
sized bulbs and vase forms, others were corona-shaped, the lower
ring suspended by chains from a small canopy-like top. Graceful

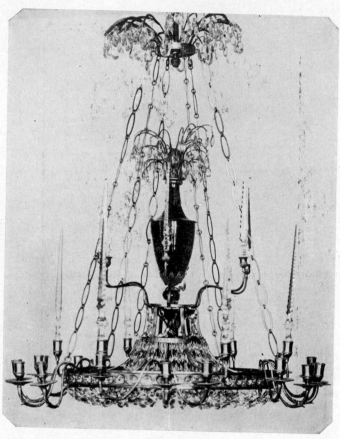

95. An Adam *lustre* with tall spires on its corona, and on curved branches attached to the pedestal which holds a beautiful blue glass vase. Courtesy French
& Co.

ovoid vases or classic urns with crystal spires were supported
above these pierced *ormolu* coronas from which the candle
branches sprang, and which often supported very tall spires.
Great ingenuity was shown in festooning these chandeliers and in
the placing of the cut glass spires.

Nothing is much lovelier than these corona chandeliers with vases and spires. One example has a circular corona similar to that in Fig. 95, but the crystal strings do not shape into a pedestal for the vase, but hang from a metal circle raised above a large blue glass bowl which holds a spraying bouquet as in Fig. 95. From the center of the bouquet ascends a long spire topped with blue glass and supporting another tiny floral bouquet. There are no other spires however. The chains depend from quite a large rectangular corona near the top, which is pierced and hung with strings of crystals as is the lower corona. The small top canopy is crown-shaped and enriched by a bouquet but lighter and with fewer sprays than that in Fig. 95.

With all their looking backward through the eyes of Pompeii to ancient Rome and Greece, the Adam Brothers were up-to-date in their use of oil lamps. They designed handsome lamps singly or in pairs. Hanging lamps largely took the place of lanterns even before the 19th Century in halls, passages, and lobbies, and were hung between the columns in formal rooms. Adam's designs are very fanciful, and to his vase, urn, and bowl motifs are added dolphins and other classic decorations, or he followed the Egyptian vogue. Brass, bronze, and glass were the chief materials. Standing lamps were placed on tables or pedestals. One of Adam's drawings made in 1773 is for a five foot lamp standard. Heppelwhite also designed some acceptable lamps, and by the end of the Century the Argand lamp was not only in general use but was admitted to high society.

Although hanging lamps ordinarily took the place of the older lanterns with candle branches, such lanterns were still seen. Whether of iron or brass, the metal framing was light; the lanterns hexagonal or octagonal; and often topped by a metal crown, vase, or flower spray suggestive of older models. Candle brackets were still placed on furniture for convenience, especially on mirror frames.

A certain pompous manner prevailed in the silverware of the early 19th Century. Candlesticks reproduced earlier styles or were designed in the modes of the day but with great elaboration. There were handsome foliated patterns with baluster stems and shaped nozzles, chased with flowers and scrolls, like those of 1814 by John and Thomas Settle. Sheffield Plate was made with the stem a clustered column about 1820, the base quadrangular and raised

96. This Waterford glass garniture in the Empire style was made about 1800. Courtesy French & Co.

on feet. A great many plated candlesticks had large painted glass shades, sometimes of thickly frosted glass. Candlesticks and candelabra abandoned delicacy for massive effects, often heavy and sometimes clumsy. Heavy fringes of glass prisms belong to the Empire period. Clumsy when poorly done they can be sumptuous when well designed. The cutting of the glass in a Waterford garniture of this type (Fig. 96) is superb. The base of the candelabrum is very finely made in a typical Empire design. It is enlightening to see what can be done with this type of fixture when we recall the atrocities which marred the beauty of many an American parlor mantel in the Federal period.

Glass candlesticks, almost as elaborate as candelabra, were embellished with metal mounts and Wedgwood bases, and had glass stems, *bobèches*, and pendants. Occasionally a bronze candlestick was made in the 16th Century manner. The candelabra branches of the early 19th Century were comparatively straight. One of silver-gilt, 1805, over three feet high, made for seven lights in two tiers, is of Egyptian inspiration; its shaft is formed of mummies with three heads and feet, base triangular, supported on winged sphinxes; decorated with foliated scrolling, lions' masks, and dolphins' heads. The craving for what we might call pretty, fancy, ladylike ornament is well expressed in a fine pair of candelabra (Fig. 97) by R. Garrard made in 1838, the successful handling of which goes far to vindicate this florid trend. Foliage and flower ornament were popular in silver and Sheffield Plate, and detachable branches were still used. An *épergne* of Sheffield Plate has candle nozzles that can be replaced by dishes, a not uncommon arrangement.

Chandeliers of Waterford glass were still made, but the Waterford works closed in 1851. Glass chandeliers made from about 1825–50 were apt to be elaborate, though there were earlier simple models. The architect, J. B. Papworth, made some designs with long oblong pendants which supplanted those of oval diamond shape. Fantastic hanging lights were occasionally conceived in the Chinese mode with all the extravagance of modern oriental taste, and held either lamps or candles; the glass pendants of many colors. Chandeliers of wood or bronze were appropriately designed for fine houses, and might carry as many as twenty-four lights. While some were conservative, others reflected the desire for novelty characteristic of the taste of the Regency (1810–20). Percier's designs influenced some of the Regency lamps made in the form of wide shallow bowls suspended by chains, ornamented with winged female figures holding vases. The marked influence of the French Directoire and Empire styles, however, could not stay the modern craving for novelty which upset and disturbed the taste of the 19th Century; but the efforts of various new schools of art failed to establish any important style.

97. The ornate character of 19th Century work is at its best in this silver candelabrum made by R. Garrard in 1838. Courtesy Crichton & Co.

CHAPTER XI

AMERICAN—COLONIAL

LIGHTING fixtures used in America in Colonial days were very provincial. Few master craftsmen left their European workshops to hazard life in the wilderness. What was fine was imported until after a century and a half of semiseparation from Europe, this country became both independent and self-reliant with the establishment of its own Federal Government. Then the work of our craftsmen took on a truly American character.

Colonial fixtures have the simplicity and naïveté often found in an untutored effort to fit the thing to the need, and their very simplicity is their charm. The subject is broad and touches many lands in the 17th and 18th Centuries: England foremost in Virginia and New England, and later in New York; Holland in New York, New Jersey, and Pennsylvania; Spain in Florida and California; and France in Louisiana. So England, Holland, Spain, and France add their quotas. So thoroughly did the influence of the Italian Renaissance and Baroque spread throughout Europe, however, that there is perhaps as much similarity as difference between European objects of any art pretension made in the 17th Century. But art had as little influence on European cottage furnishings as on those of America, and the common fixtures, the open oil lamp and the rushlight holder were similar on both continents during the 17th and the 18th Centuries.

Candles were luxuries here, and candlesticks if beautiful belonged to the homes of the rich. In the 17th Century fine Colonial houses were supplied with imported silver and brass candlesticks, and in the late 17th Century with sconces of various kinds. In the 18th Century, candelabra, sconces, chandeliers, and lanterns of different materials were imported quite freely from England and the Continent. But America was distinctly and still is the home of the lamp. Although kerosene replaced fish oil, lard oil and grease,

226 PERIOD LIGHTING FIXTURES

as well as sperm oil and camphene, only to be replaced by gas and electricity, still the lamp form has never been abandoned and to-day has multiplied.

The primitive open oil pan for a floating wick was the lamp common to Italy, Spain, France, and America. At some point in its use here it was called a Betty lamp, possibly as is claimed, by corrupting the German word *besser* meaning *better*, as applied to the covered oil pan which was better than the open one. The iron Betty lamp is given a Mayflower pedigree. But not long after the Pilgrims' landing, iron was discovered here and Betty lamps were cast or wrought. Later they were made of tin and took on different local characteristics as in the "Ipswich Betty," and the "Newburyport Betty." They were attached to a stand like a candlestick, with or without a handle; placed on a low stand; or hung on an adjustable ratchet. The oil pan was variously shaped: a small round shallow saucer; a flat plate of metal turned up on four sides with four corners for wicks; sometimes rather nicely shaped with a little lip, nose, or open spout for a single wick; or box-shaped with vertical sides.

The Spanish *candil* and the French *candile* are as nearly related to our Betty lamp as is the speech of each of these nations, derived from the Latin mother tongue. Even the double oil pan calculated to save the drippings was a European as well as an American economy. But the comparison of these primitive forms is more of a study for the antiquarian than a subject of general interest. While very little was ordinarily done to decorate these early American lamps, their shapes are their chief attraction and often show nice instinct for form and outline. Those with a single lip opposite the handle (Figs. 98, 99) seem to offer the greatest possibility for fine shaping, and many of this type are far from primitive in their modeling. Some are elongated so that their sides slope gradually toward the wick projection or lip. Others pinch in more or less sharply, as does a spout on a pitcher, and give occasion for some good smithing. The curve of the wick spout is often excellently conceived, evidence that we had some good smiths in the country at this time. The shaping of these spouts is as interesting to collectors as is that of pitchers which they often resemble. The vertical handle too gave some scope for design. There is the flat broad handle that ends in a good fat trefoil resembling a cross (Fig. 98), or maybe only in a double scallop. Others, and these are the most common, end in a forward bend (Fig. 99) so that the

98. Open iron oil cups with lips for the wick, or closed with a wick tube, served the early Colonists in the 17th Century. Courtesy The Metropolitan Museum.

lamp may hang plumb in a horizontal position. These handles vary greatly in length, breadth, and shape. Some bend sharply, others turn in an easy curve, which gives them some distinction. As simple as they are, collectors prize these Betty lamps for their individuality, and they do possess this quality.

We are reminded how barren were the lives of the majority of the early Colonists when we compare their oil lamps with 15th

Century Continental examples of the same type, to say nothing of the beautiful Roman lamps. As early as the 15th Century every part of the lamp was ornamented. Its surface was covered with beautiful design. Its fixed handle was shaped elaborately, often broadening considerably and covered with surface ornament; and even its hanging bar was knopped, ringed, or otherwise decorated.

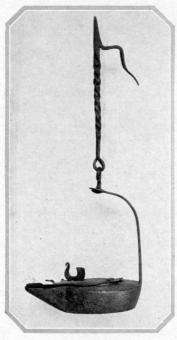

99. A very nice example of a 17th Century covered iron Betty lamp with a combination spike and hook for convenient hanging. Courtesy The Metropolitan Museum.

There is a fine example in the Cluny Museum in Paris. In America we find little effort at embellishment, but we do find some. In a covered lamp (Fig. 99) a tiny scrolled bird serves as handle on the cover. The hanging rod tapers nicely toward the bottom and is ornamented by twisting. The hook near the top is quite sophisticated proclaiming a master hand, for the hooks on ordinary examples (Fig. 98) are far more simple.

The pointed hanging bar of the Betty lamp is not a new idea either. At least as early as the 15th Century and doubtless far earlier this same kind of a bar was used for similar lamps. It was stuck horizontally into some convenient wooden beam or chink in the masonry, so that the lamp itself swung at right angles far away from the beam or wall. The sharp pointed hook near its end was calculated for various purposes: to hang from a rail or rack, a shelf, or any projection, so as to give sufficient swing to the lamp.

In our Colonies these lamps were probably used at the fireside, as they were evil smelling things at best, least offensive near a chimney where the smoke could escape. Candles though considered a luxury when used in any quantity were not uncommon in thrifty households, and rushlights were probably more general than candles especially in the early days. Of course many stand ards, most of them low, were made to set these lamps above the table-top at a convenient height, proving that they were used for other work or for more general lighting. But the housewife would nevertheless find the hanging rod useful as a handle around the large kitchen fireplace as she peered into her deep pot or searched her cupboard. In covered lamps, the wick might project through a hole in the top (Fig. 98). Those with a double oil pan, one placed below to catch drippings, are the Phœbe lamps. The covers were hinged or sliding. A lamp used in the late 17th Century, about 1692 in Salem, was whimsically shaped like a cup and saucer with spouts projecting from both.

The striking point in examining any great number of these early lamps is their variety and ingenuity, two distinctively American traits early evident in American workmanship. Earliest examples were of iron, then of tin—and these were used well into the 19th Century, later of pewter, copper, brass, earthenware—though rarely of earthenware. The tin Betty lamp might set in a tray of sand called a "Tidy-top," designed to catch the dripping oil. To raise the light the lamp was placed on a low stand with baluster stem like the English wooden stands for candlesticks so beautifully elaborated in mahogany in the late Rococo period. The Colonial examples were of native wood, often maple, but when the lamp was of tin the stand might also be of tin, more convenient than shapely. Lamps of tin or pewter had different shaped oil containers—cylindrical or flat sided, set on a stem or directly on a pan, with or without handles. One or two wick spouts were variously placed, finally on the top. Bases varied according to fancy;

100. Rushlight holders were similar in the 17th and 18th Centuries on both sides of the Atlantic. This 18th Century example of iron has a good wooden base and a sprightly up-curve to the unattached rod. Courtesy The Metropolitan Museum.

one with a sugar-loaf base called a "petticoat-lamp," some with a peg socket underneath the skirt which might be fitted on to the upright of a chair.

The rushlight holder (Fig. 100) was early made of wrought-iron, simply contrived for utility with little effort at embellishment except that the heavy wooden base might be nicely molded. Imported candlesticks were of Renaissance and Baroque types—

Jacobean, Restoration, and William-and-Mary, if English. It must be remembered that the English early took over New York and set the styles. Toward the end of the Century silver candlesticks were cast in baluster form. Many were undecorated, depending for beauty on their form and material. Those with tubular tops usually had removable nozzles. Some were of cluster column type. One made by Jeremiah Dummer of Boston is formed like eight engaged columns shaped square, with a square projecting nozzle. A similar projection, reminiscent of the grease pan low on the stem, is placed just above the circular foot on its square molded base. Dummer worked well into the 18th Century but this candlestick is an earlier model. The so-called "Mayflower candlestick" is the ringed type with tubular stem and round base with a large grease pan set low on the stem. Candlesticks were of iron, tin, or pewter; the pewter quite plain. But little pewter remains, as it was run into bullets during the Revolution. Iron candlesticks occasionally had a lip to hang on a chair.

Candle stands for the floor (Figs. 101 and 102), which were so well made in the 18th Century, seem to have been used to some extent in the 17th. These were of wrought-iron and possibly also of wood, occasionally with a screw stem to adjust the candle branches, and with tripod feet. One example of wood which claims a 17th Century origin has a circular shelf on the stem evidently used as a work-table.

Hoop lights with candle sockets were hung from the ceiling, a very primitive type of chandelier. Lanterns hung in halls and entries. Glass for windows was imported very early in the history of the Colonies even when its use was far from general in England, but we have not yet found any record of its use in these very early American-made lanterns. Hand lanterns were fitted with horn as in early English examples. It seems quite possible that the entry lanterns were imported as they often were in the 18th Century.

With the 18th Century came leisure to embellish local handicraft. Silver, pewter, iron, tin, wood, glass, and pottery were worked into fixtures in the changing fashions of the day, inspired by European models, often with independence and individuality but more often with a naïveté and complete ignorance of art forms and motifs. The baluster stem, reminiscent of the composite stem of classic vase and urn forms of the Italian Renaissance, in the hands of Early American craftsmen lacking a European art train-

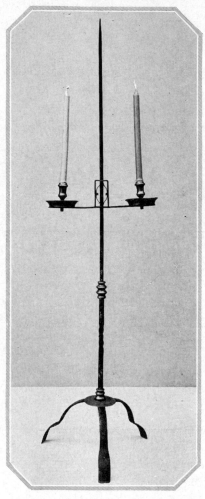

101. The 18th Century iron candle stand is a delightful contrivance with its adjustable horizontal bar to raise or lower the lights. Courtesy The Metropolitan Museum.

ing, showed an ignorance of design often resulting in dispropor-
tion or exaggeration. This is especially noticeable in the elongated
urn form of the nozzle.

Open and covered iron Betty lamps were used for every-day

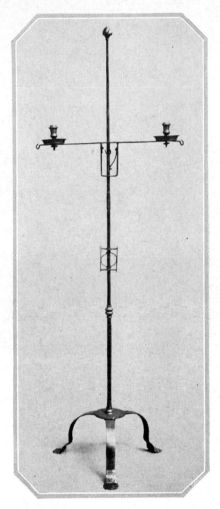

102. The voluted tripod feet in this 18th Century candle stand are excellently
designed, as are the brass knob, finial, and candle holders. An unnecessary arm
brace later added to the standard. Courtesy The Metropolitan Museum.

lighting; tin was common, but pewter and glass were preferred. One or two glass lenses or bull's eyes were sometimes fixed to a lamp to increase the light for work or reading. Glass, though of poor quality, was made as early as 1750 at Quincy, Massachusetts, where several types of lamps were manufactured with a twisted spiral in the stem and perhaps in the handle.

There is an engaging variety in these early lamps, whether a little spark or "sparking" lamp, which burned only a short time, useful for inns and popular for courting or "sparking" as it was called; the squat or typical tavern lamp; squat chamber lamps of many kinds; peg lamps to fit conveniently into a candlestick; petticoat lamps; time lamps with glass reservoirs marked to note the hours by night; shop, store, or factory lamps; marine or whaler's lamps swung on pivots to right themselves at sea, sometimes made with a ring on the circular foot to hang on the wall at sea or at home. Glass and pewter were rivals for favor, but glass finally superseded metal. Their shapes are often gracious and pleasing: sometimes set upon baluster or tubular standards like candlesticks, or set directly on a dish-like foot or slightly above it. Their fonts were shaped like a goblet, acorn, drum; were bulbous, vase, urn, mug, or inverted bell-shape, or almost any shape that would hold the oil. Some were furnished with long well modeled side handles often reaching far down on the stem, or small circular or scrolled handles; while others were handleless; and not a few variously equipped for hanging. Chamber lamps were apt to be fitted with a ring on the dished foot opposite the handle and hung conveniently on the wall.

Imported lamps were luxuries and naturally were of the finer sort, glass especially. In 1773 a New York dealer advertised "very rich cut glass lamps—globe or barrel" shaped. But earlier in the mid-Century glass chamber lamps had been frequently imported. Both England and France supplied dining-room table lamps set up on well modeled standards of brass, bronze, or glass, sometimes decoratively hung with glass pendants. Whale oil was in general use although various greases like lard and other animal fats supplied the Betty lamps. In 1763 the flat wick came into use which is still the ordinary lamp wick.

Candlesticks were of baluster type; occasionally with an oval base. The simple tubular stems were for common use. Tin, brass, and pewter took the place of the earlier iron tubular stems or the simple prickets or sockets set on a stem with three or four feet, the iron occasionally boasting a few ornamental twists. Here is the origin of the design for those delightful iron candle stands which have not been bettered to-day. They are one of the most pleasing of 18th and 19th Century fixtures (Figs. 101, 102), arranged ordinarily with an adjustable horizontal cross-beam with a candle socket on either end. They frequently had snuffers and extinguishers conveniently hung on their framework and might be further embellished with brass knobs.

If there is any fixture of this Colonial period over which we are tempted to wax eloquent, and it is hard to do so with Italy, Spain, France, and even England in mind, it is the candle stand. It seems to us the most acceptable of the early fixtures. Its simplicity is of course its charm. It was most practical too. The adjustable candle arm to raise and lower the light was a nice contrivance, and the arrangement of the spring which held it in place on the standard gave its maker an occasion for a somewhat ornamental motif in an indispensable element of the fixture. The vertical rod was topped by a spike or a finial. The knops on this rod were often of brass and gave some latitude for elaboration. But the tripod feet remain the true theme for the designer. These are simply achieved, usually with broad flat strips of metal which widen and spread on the floor or which barely contact it. The slight volute in the foot proves these tripods to be many centuries away from their vigorous Romanesque ancestry of France, Spain, and Italy, yet more like them than unlike. Some tripods are formed of angular rods which taper to a rat's-tail along the floor and have no hint of a volute. Even the broad strap-metal is not always voluted, and the stem may show a nice twisting. Some tripods are low and form a broad segment of a circle as they curve downward with a sharp bend at the foot. There are odd and curious examples, freak pieces valued by collectors but of no importance in the evolution of the fixture. England had a way of making her candle stands for both rushlights or candles so that a single stand could be used for either. The rushlight holder was like a pair of pincers. Many English 18th Century examples had heavy wooden bases either domed like a hemisphere or simply cross-beamed with the ends slanting and occasionally nicely molded. These carried single adjustable arms to raise and lower the light, and might add a folding hinge contrivance to lengthen the arm, if there were only one arm. There are American examples of this type made in wood. The finials in American candle stands might be anything from a knob or acorn to a very primitive cock like the village wearthercock. There was doubtless little difference between English and American examples of this simple fixture made by English smiths on both sides of the Atlantic. Snuffers were more generally used in this 18th Century, and they were accommodated by little hooks on the candle stand, which were located at different points on the bracing of the candle arm. To balance the snuffers, another hook was placed on the opposite side for the little cone used as an extinguisher. The horizontal candle arm was variously finished at either end. Often the *bobèche* was set on its extremity (Fig. 101), or it extended beyond the grease pan and terminated in a small hook for snuffers on one side and extinguisher on the other (Fig. 102). More sophisticated examples however ended in a downward curve which was purely ornamental; sometimes small and trim, sometimes bold and full, and sometimes sprawling and crude. In one example the arm itself is spread sufficiently to hold the candle socket without a grease pan. Many ingenious ideas were worked out in these candle stands. They will bear considerable study, for the same idea was further used in the candelabrum. It is clear to see that Washington's brass candelabrum (Fig. 103) is but a variant of this idea. The bracing of the candle arm on the candle stand later became much elongated and elaborated; and in place of the small rectangular element (Figs. 101 and 102), the bracing reached far out on the candle arm and was the chief decorative motif of the piece. Rush-light holders were still in use with bases variously formed of wood or iron. Even tin was occasionally used cone-fashion as a base, especially for a candle stand.

Candlesticks of brass, if not of silver, seem to us to-day typically Colonial, and many were in use. Silver was for the parlor and

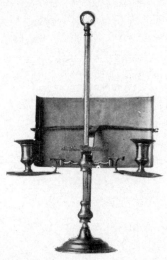

103. This brass candelabrum with a reflector was used during the Revolution by Washington in the President's house in Philadelphia and at Mount Vernon. A 21-inch steel rod supports the adjustable candle holders, each being a complete chamber candlestick. Courtesy United States National Museum.

dining room in fine houses, brass for other rooms, and pewter or tin for the kitchen and servants. Pewter and tin, with an occasional pair in brass, served the cottage. Early pieces of pewter were often home-made but from about 1750 there were a number of prominent makers of pewter ware and candlesticks were not uncommon. Imported candlesticks were used in fashionable homes and many a letter was sent to England and France with orders for the latest things in "candleware." English silver and Sheffield Plate appeared with faceted or turned baluster forms of the various period styles: William-and-Mary, Queen Anne, and Georgian, if English; Louis XIV and XV, if French. Georgian styles were preëminent.

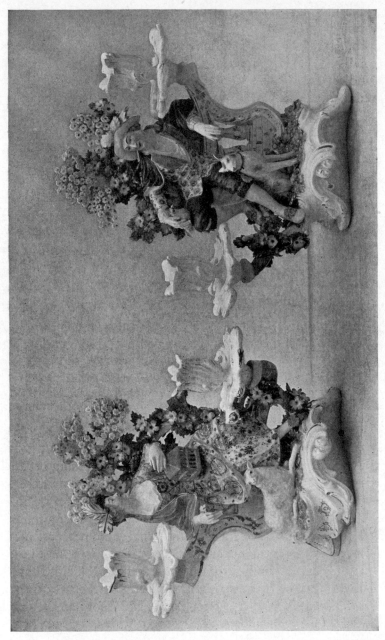

IX. These Chelsea porcelain arbour candelabra were as much in vogue in America as in England. This pair is notable for its vigorous Rococo character and beautiful coloring. Made about 1760. From the collection of Lord Leverhulme. Courtesy The Anderson Galleries.

Early Georgian, Rococo, and the classical styles of the Brothers Adam followed with no very great delay. Candlesticks were made of glass cut or molded in ornamental shapes; English pottery; Chelsea (Fig. IX) and other porcelain in figures, especially with rustic settings; enameled and japanned for the toilet and tea tables, and japanned chamber candlesticks in green, red, black, and gilt. Candle screens and shades too were not unknown. Even tortoise-shell, and *Vernis Martin* were none too fine for the splendid homes of the late Colonial period. Wood was doubtless used more than seems evident from the antiques which the early 19th Century spared. Candlesticks of mahogany in the Chippendale style were at least known.

There was a variety of designs from which to choose one's candlesticks, and when the splendid big glass hurricane shade covered candlestick and candle to protect it from the draft in the hallway, a highly decorative element was added to the impressive Colonial house. These hurricane shades were variously ornamented in floral designs. The New Jersey and Pennsylvania glass works were in operation from about the mid-Century so that Stiegel and Wistar glass were not uncommon. Candlesticks of colored glass had something of a vogue. If Stiegel, perhaps that rich bluish to red amethyst, blue, or purple with elongated tubular nozzle. If Wistar, it might have a baluster stem in vase form of pale green glass. It is pleasant to contemplate that a plain peacock-blue glass bowl from Wistar's works, originally procurable for a few pennies, recently sold at auction for $800.

Candelabra and girandoles were often imported and followed the European styles—French and English. In 1762 we note a pair of four-armed cut glass girandoles decorated with stars and pendants.

Wall brackets especially in pairs were used to a certain extent but handsome sconces were apt to be imported. There were a few wood-carvers here in America in the 17th Century and in the early 18th Century they possibly turned their hands to carving some backplates for sconces. Simple ones were made here we know, often of tin. The early forms were long and narrow with clipped corners at the top or a simple crimped or scalloped crest hinting the fine shell cresting of Queen Anne models. The candle was set in a socket in a small semicircular tray at the bottom of the long narrow wall-plate. Other wall-plates were circular or oval and were occasionally ornamented with star centers and other motifs. Much ingenuity is shown in these 18th Century sconces. Some are of

104. This chandelier with its gilded wood baluster and metal candle arms, made 1750–75, resembles the English brass chandeliers of the early 18th Century. Courtesy The Metropolitan Museum.

pewter with a pattern of large and small circular reflectors, some are mirror backed. Convex mirrors in circular frames with candle brackets were in great vogue as early as 1730. Flat oval and rectangular mirrors were similarly framed. These frames were of mahogany, walnut, or gilt, sometimes white, always ornamental. Dressing glasses were often handsomely japanned.

Brass or glass chandeliers were not common in the American Colonial home. Such chandeliers as had any artistic pretension were imported. Simple hoops, coronas, or cross-beams—candle-beams, were used in the 17th Century. Provincial adaptations of the European carved wood chandeliers had good gadrooning and simple ornament. Some were made with heavy vase-like stems of wood and simply scrolled though vivacious arms with crimped *bobèches* for the candles. That some craftsmen were familiar with European work, or obtained European designs and were skillful enough to follow them, is proved by an excellent chandelier (Fig. 104) with six candle branches made between the years 1750 and 1775. It closely resembles an English chandelier (Fig. 86) made

105. Much labor was occasionally expended on the pierced designs of 18th Century cylindrical lanterns, with or without a glassed front; while rectangular ones were often plain. Courtesy The Metropolitan Museum.

of brass in the early 18th Century. The American example has the baluster stem of wood, carved and gilded, while the branches are of metal. It has a large knopped middle member, reminiscent of the classic jar forms, to which the candle branches are attached. Above and below are nicely shaped motifs, both gadrooned. The finial is carved in a conventional flame motif somewhat resembling a tulip. The metal candle branches swing out in easy reversed curves and terminate in flaring *bobèches* with long tubular sockets.

The lantern was purely utilitarian with the early Colonists. A lantern might be hung in the entry or in a hallway, but even in the 18th Century few attained elegance. Both horn and glass were used for translucence but the tin lantern was the ordinary type. There are many quaint examples of 18th Century workmanship—cylindrical, and rectangular, or polygonal, with tops varying from the simple cone to forms reminiscent of the turret lanterns of Italy and Spain.

Lanterns were nothing to brag of from the art point of view at this time (Fig. 105), when the Italian lantern had perfected its cycle of beauty, while the Spanish lantern was at its zenith,

106. This 18th Century iron lantern is a highly provincial rendering of a Renaissance type with a fanciful lily-crowned turret. Courtesy The Metropolitan Museum.

the French lantern coming into its own, and even the English lantern not altogether a negligible quantity. In examining any number of these early lanterns we find echoes though often faint, of European types (Fig. 106) long ago perfected and beautifully embellished. This too brings us face to face with the stern facts of ordinary Colonial living in the 17th and early 18th Centuries, for even the elaborate pierced designs in old tin lanterns belong more generally to the Federal period than to the Colonial, although many were made at this time.

Imported lanterns were of several kinds. In the mid-18th Century "barrel and bell glass lanthorns for entries" were advertised. There were square and spherical or globe lanterns for halls and stairways in standard sizes, 18 x 14 inches, 16 x 12, 10 x 14, 9 x 4, 8 x 4, 7 x 4. There was an occasional lantern of Renaissance type, hexagonal with sides tapering toward the bottom, but of little artistic pretension though hung in a mansion. It was not until Federal times and then only sporadically that the lantern had any considerable attention from designers. Early lanterns were little more than candle protectors. Later oil lamps were used in them. But neither the lantern, nor the candlestick appealed to American ingenuity and resourcefulness as did the lamp, the candelabrum, and the chandelier which under Federal rule developed many interesting variants of the Continental styles. Ingenuity rather than art, clever adaptation rather than real originality marked the lighting fixtures of Colonial America.

CHAPTER XII

AMERICAN—FEDERAL

ALTHOUGH a new spirit pervaded our Early Republic, we were willing to take our fashions from the Adam Brothers in England, and the Directorate and Empire in France. The classic styles of Rome and Pompeii fitted into popular thinking, which was a bit bombastic and sentimental in print and politics, however commonplace in everyday affairs.

After the Revolution the young Republic tried heroically to stand on its own legs. They strutted a bit to support the popular thinking of the day, but after all they fell back into their accustomed gait and affairs went on about as usual. The lighting fixtures were not so different from those of Continental days except that the country grew and prospered, and with prosperity came increased luxury in the home. Chandeliers and sconces were more generally used, lamps were improved, and candleware—especially candelabra for the mantel garniture, became the pride of the household. In the last quarter of the 18th Century patriotism waxed strong and the eagle flapped his wings quite vigorously in household decoration and ornament. But Sheraton and Adam were household words, and there was no strut to them at all, only a stately beauty that one could live with and be wholly self-respecting. The styles of the French Directorate and Empire were welcomed and held their ground with much dignity until the ornate lady-like furnishings peculiar to Queen Victoria's régime found their way over the water.

The successive style influences we find in the lighting fixtures of our Federal period are: late Georgian, running concurrently with the furniture styles of Shearer, Sheraton, Heppelwhite, and Adam; French Directoire and Empire. Then came the Victorian era; after which arrived the pale days of the *pastel, art nouveau,* and finally the splendor of modern lighting and the glory of mod-

244

ern fixtures embracing every period and country of the civilized world.

Until the late 19th Century Americans were so keen for new things—novelty, changing fashions, and most of all improvement and progress that old things were not merely discarded but were either destroyed or abandoned as rubbish even when stowed away in attic, cellar, or barn. So that antiques rescued from abandoned trash heaps have little hope of being accurately dated except as scraps of definite information are picked up here and there and tabulated. The nearest approach to accuracy in dating such antiques is seldom by decade, or even quarter-century, but more often "late 18th or early 19th Century" is the nearest approach to classification which has yet been attempted.

Metal and glass candlesticks were more common than pottery ones. Designs in the 18th and early 19th Century were innumerable, ranging from plain tubular stems to elaborate baluster types. Silver, plated silver, pewter, brass, bronze, white metal, and tin; glass, clear and colored; and pottery all went to their making, with the occasional appearance of something unusual, especially in the early 19th Century, like a pair in alabaster or the more usual mahogany ones so popular in England. Imported candlesticks, far from being disdained, were objects of pride. The possession of a fine pair made of tortoise-shell, like those now in the Cooper Union collection, or finished in *Vernis Martin*—the famous French varnish, was occasion for boasting. Bronze candlesticks, especially of Adam design, with the characteristic tapering pedestal shaft and urn top, were imported and highly valued, particularly for the library. Other models executed in bronze had a cylindrical stem on a molded base, or a tapering shaft with a tulip *bobèche* and a square molded base.

Brass candlesticks were in general use, pewter less common, silver for the dining-table and elsewhere in great houses. In the early 19th Century wicks were thick and required snuffers which were finished to match the candlestick and placed on an ornamental tray. The newer hard wicks needed little snuffing. In the early Federal period we find very provincial renderings of a well-known French and English candlestick in a tall elongated vase form on a high foot, sometimes set on an oblong rectangular base. Candlesticks, with nozzle set directly on the base as in Europe, were for chamber use; stemmed candlesticks for other rooms. For economy a spring device inside a tubular or column stem, sometimes an unusually tall stem at that, was used in the cheaper sort of candlesticks. Candle nozzles were not infrequently in the classic urn form favored in Europe, and the stems were often the classic column.

Early brass candlesticks were apt to be of Colonial type. Some were ring-turned with a ring handle and bar thumb support. There were many pleasing designs. The spreading cylindrical or knopped stems were prominent. A graceful knopped stem flares into a bell foot on a square base with chamfered corners. A slender shaft spreads into a circular base. A ringed baluster stem is set on a square base with canted corners or on an oblong base with rounded corners. Tapering ringed and baluster shafts are placed on square bases with canted corners. Columns have classic urn nozzles. A circular pedestal sets on a circular base. Pan candlesticks have circular dishes with up-curved rim and flat horizontal handles sometimes decorated with *repoussé* acanthus ornament. Heights varied, usually from seven to nine inches; but many were made low, and many were hung with glass pendants for mantel garnitures accompanying a large middle candelabrum or a clock.

Silver candlesticks were apt to be quite plain, with column or baluster stems, the column occasionally with an oblong grease pan and foot like one made by Isaac Hutton in Albany (1790–1800). Later, fancy stopped at nothing and we find such rustic and patriotic pieces as a naturalistic representation of the historic Oak tree on Boston Common, with carefully modeled trunk and leaves on a heavy base.

Britannia ware was introduced about 1825, and this with japanned tin ware took the place of pewter. But an odd piece was occasionally made of pewter, perhaps with a turned stem on a molded base; or a bell-shaped base with a grease pan just above it.

One pair (Fig. 107), with a tall slender shaft and high molded base, shows how far afield the designer had wandered from the approved Georgian models. The stem is elongated nearly one-third more than the usual baluster form. It is an interesting variant, but it teases the eye trained to the proportions of accepted types. Pick it to pieces, and there are many good elements. The vase motif of the stem is not bad, and the base is excellent, so is the candle socket. But the whole candlestick looks as if it had been drawn out to reach a required height.

107. This tall pewter candlestick shows the provincial handling of the baluster shaft. 18th Century. Courtesy The Anderson Galleries.

Tin was in common use for the kitchen, and even chamber and student's candlesticks. An upright student's candle-lamp has an adjustable shade and stand; a square center rod is fitted into a deep saucer base, the candle nozzle is attached to the rod by a neatly curved bracket. One example dating about 1816–20 is nicely made, with a convenient handle topping the rod. White metal might be used for an early chamber candlestick, with molded lip, scroll handle, urn *bobèche*, and a conical extinguisher. Mica chimneys for candles are of later date and were used on tin or brass candlesticks which were sometimes conveniently made with a broad saucer base, the candle on one side and a match box on the other. China was rare. Wedgwood was imported, but usually in garnitures.

The Wedgwood ornament was generally used in the circular portion of the pedestal. It was made in a cylinder several inches wide and formed part of the base of the candlestick or the candelabrum. One set of candlesticks (Fig. 108), called variously candelabra and *lustres* because of their ornate character, has this Wedgwood element set in *ormolu* on a circular molded base. The

108. *Ormolu*, Wedgwood, and crystal embellish this pair of 18th Century candelabra *"lustres."* Courtesy The Metropolitan Museum.

pottery is decorated in a white raised design on a blue ground. This jasper of Wedgwood's was famous and was made on a green, as well as on blue, lilac, and many other colored grounds. The design is classic, with medallions in each of which are figure groups. Each medallion is bordered, and a classic border edges the cylinder at top and bottom. The fixture is designed to hold a single candle. The domed base of the stem sets on this pedestal much as if it were a candlestick. Just above the base is a large oval knop of crystal elaborately cut, above which is placed a wide scalloped crystal *bobèche* hung with strings of crystal pendants. The urn-shaped candle socket, also of cut crystal, has a flaring edge from which hang shorter strings of pendants. Though a bit heavy looking, such ornaments were in keeping with the mantel garnitures of the day and were thought extremely elegant as they were in the latest mode. Similar candlesticks or *lustres*, as our great-grandmothers preferred to call them, were all of glass and were sometimes of better proportion though of similar design. One pair of clear glass has a base like the short cut-column of the Empire style. From this rises the stem: first a cut glass ball, and then a nicely tapering shaft to uphold the well-proportioned saucer-shaped *bobèche* from which long strings of pendants are hung. The sockets flare, not widely but with a hint of the cornucopia model typical of Empire designs.

Glass had only recently become really plentiful and it was used a great deal but never more effectively than in the hurricane shades. These big hurricane shades (Fig. 109), practical in hallways to protect the candle flame from drafts, especially in big Southern halls with open doors at front and back, are objects of high decorative value. Nothing is more suitable in a hallway furnished in the Federal style than a pair of these fine old glass shades when appropriately placed on a good table or console. They are either plain or ornamented with the floral designs characteristic of the taste of the day, often incorporating a spread-eagle.

Porcelain was made here in the 19th Century, and pottery continued in use. The mottled Bennington ware from Vermont became quite popular. This pottery was established in 1793 by John Norton of Revolutionary fame, and closed in 1858. Candlesticks ordinarily had columnar stems on cylindrical spreading feet. This ware even in the 18th Century was made in rich colorings, mottled in brown, yellow, cream, and dull green. Touches of dull blue and red are occasionally found. Candlesticks were both low and tall with column or baluster stems, molded nozzle and round foot. Some of them were heavy and clumsy, though the tall tubular ones were well formed. They were accepted for cottage use but were not at home with fine crystal, Wedgwood, and *ormolu*. Other wares, of the types made in Baltimore, Trenton, etc., have much more elaborate baluster stems, classic urn nozzles, and high pierced bases.

109. Pairs of ornamented hurricane shades, tall enough to overtop both candle-stick and candle, were highly decorative. Early 19th Century. Courtesy The Metropolitan Museum.

Glass candlesticks were legion; plain and colored, fancy and simple, cut and molded in many forms. These were not always locally made. They might be of imported Waterford glass or colored glass from Bohemia. But glass was early made here. Wistar was the first American maker of flint glass. From his New Jersey works he supplied his customers with candlesticks in the colors popular in the late years of the Colonies and in fact until 1780. Dark blue, clear green, pale green, amber, and yellow were favorites and were made in good baluster patterns with vase-shaped stems.

There were other glass-works, following the closing of the Stiegel works of Colonial fame, but the products of none are so well known to-day as is the Sandwich glass. The works where this glass was made started operating in 1825 and made some candlesticks but more lamps. Glass candlesticks were of many colors and in a variety of shapes: deep blue, ringed column, vase socket, square base; turquoise blue dolphin, with milk-white tulip socket; blue column on a star-shaped base; spiral fluted stem, on octagonal base, urn socket; baluster stem, tapered and fluted, gadrooned, scalloped base in hobnail pattern, urn top; Directoire patterns, flower and matted urn top, scrolled triangular base; molded stepped quatrefoil and urn top; canary yellow, baluster, with a scalloped base; turquoise blue opaque, hexagonal stem and base; column with spreading nozzle, molded jar form in center stem, spreading foot stepped and molded. Dolphin candlesticks were made in ultramarine blue, vaseline yellow, etc., clear or opaque glass; the dolphin on a mound-like base with classic urn nozzle. Dolphin patterns were more graceful than those with square bases single or stepped with urn or flower nozzles. The classic forms were short, clumsy, and provincial. Occasionally the tall figure of a woman formed the stem and the nozzle was a classic urn, possibly in that opalescent glass characteristic of the Sandwich works. The earlier examples are graceful in design and have that "bright silvery texture" peculiar to Sandwich glass whether clear, colored, or opaque.

Candlesticks made in New York State were in the fashionable colors of the day: some in aquamarine blue of unusual design incorporating vase forms, provincial yet charming, the base rounded, nozzle elongated; others were short, heavy, and clumsy looking with flower nozzles; some with tall stepped bases, square or polygonal. There is considerable choice among them and occasionally there will be found a good feeling for design.

Some early glass candlesticks have saucer tops on hollow columns. One pair has an unusual ringed middle section, hexagonal stem, and molded hexagonal base. Jar forms were also used, and sometimes a sort of double base is found. An early pair in clear glass is vase-shaped with deep circular *bobèche* on turned bulbous stem, the deep base enriched with a symmetrical tear drop pattern. Amethyst glass was effective, designed in a hexagonal tapering shaft flaring into a six-sided base. Collectors prize the pieces which show holding marks made when extracting a piece from the mold, as in a pair of white glass baluster candlesticks spirally twisted with vase sockets, circular spirally gadrooned foot with scalloped edges. Elaborate candlesticks ornamented with pendants were apt to be imported. A Waterford pair is of milk-white and ruby glass, the baluster stem decorated with vertical gilt lines, spreading rims and feet, scalloped edges; the octagonal panels of ruby glass bordered with gold. A pair of Sandwich glass *lustres* has wide flaring *bobèches* like a shallow champagne glass, ornamented with long pendant prisms.

Candelabra and girandoles were still imported, though they were early made here especially for mantel garnitures in sets of two or three *lustres,*—a pair of candlesticks and one candelabrum of three or five lights. The glass prisms were imported from France more cheaply than they could be made here. Marble bases were in vogue during the early 19th Century and long continued fashionable. Early examples were simple, mere candlesticks with five or six glass prisms. From 1800 to 1825 girandoles were elaborated in brass, bronze, and various gilded metals. Figure designs were popular: idyllic and pastoral as in France and England; patriotic or sentimental showing Washington, some Indian chieftain, a viking, a pioneer, a military figure, Pocahontas, Robinson Crusoe, or Paul and Virginia; cupids and birds, vines and flowers.

A brass standard hung with pendants, on a base of marble, was the popular conception of elegance. Sometimes we find these pieces designated as "girandole candelabra." Very elaborate designs were made in later days by New York and other jewelers to meet the growing demand for elaborate ornaments as the country's wealth increased. Those in the Adam style, with garlands, pendants, and spires were very elegant.

Of all the Federal lighting fixtures none are more interesting than the wall brackets, for these ordinarily have very ornamental backplates. They were prominent decorations in the interiors of

the period and of considerable importance. They were made in
pairs and variously placed. If there is one type of sconce more
typically Federal than another it is the circular convex mirror in
a carved and gilded frame with two small scrolled candle branches
depending from it, and topped by an eagle. It will be remembered

110. An 18th Century convex mirror with candle brackets set in its carved
and gilded frame, excellently ornamented with acanthus and eagle. Courtesy
The Anderson Galleries.

that the vogue for the eagle in England started in 1790 and ran
into the Empire period, 1810.

There is considerable choice among these gilt-framed mirrors
from an artistic point of view, and not all of their frames were
accommodated with candle brackets. One very successful design
(Fig. 110) makes excellent use of the acanthus. The molding of the

frame has that plain middle band with tiny ball drops spaced at regular intervals, much in vogue at this time. A nice beading rims the glass itself, and an elaborate ornament finishes it above and below. The lower finial is an acanthus bouquet excellently designed with skill equal to that of the best European workmen. The upper ornament is a pediment enriched by an anthemion formed like a shell. On either side of this pediment are effective scrollings of acanthus leaves, and upon the pediment a finely modeled spread-eagle perches on a rock-like base. The candle branches are inconspicuous metal scrolls upholding cusped glass *bobèches* with cut glass candle urns, the edges of which spread considerably like a bowl. Long slender glass pendants hang from the *bobèches*. This is a highly successful rendering of a fashionable 18th Century English model, but other examples often lack the excellence of designing evident in this mirror frame. The ball drops were sometimes too large and illy proportioned for the frame. The acanthus bouquet was inexpertly handled, or three long water leaves might be substituted curving somewhat clumsily in a three-feathered motif from the mouth of a gadrooned vase; and the spread-eagle perched stolidly, as wooden as any Noah's ark toy, on its circular pedestal, from which two water leaves curved even more stiffly than those in the finial bouquet. Well shaped glass candle sockets and *bobèches* with short pendants might do what they could to redeem the piece, but it remained a highly provincial rendering of a fine conception. These sconces had a great vogue in the early days of the Republic and continued in fashion into the 19th Century. Mirrors in various forms composed the backplates of sconces; one type for a single candle was circular or oval, formed of small sections of silvered glass. Wall brackets were still called "branches" and were often imported. Those of brass, from London or Paris, might be lyre-shaped with two or three curved ornate brackets. French *appliques* in the current modes were occasionally used. Classic form and ornament prevailed as in the *Louis Seize* and Adam styles with glass pendants and garlands, and later in charming examples in the Directoire and Empire styles.

Sconces were often elaborately contrived of wood. One pair (Fig. 111) is carved and gilded in the Sheraton style. The back-plate is a bundle of spears bound with crossed thongs and flaring a little at the top. Upon this is placed a horizontal pediment somewhat wider than the candle branches which depend from a carved

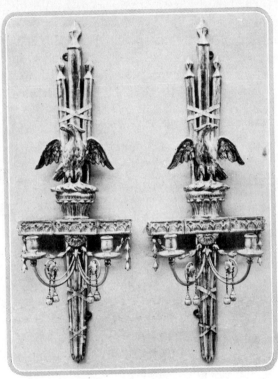

111. Sconces carved and gilded in the Sheraton style became characteristic features of well furnished rooms in the Federal period. These date from 1790–1800. Courtesy The Metropolitan Museum.

motif below it. These branches are of metal as in most of these wall brackets. Sometimes they are wholly of metal, and sometimes the tiny decorative tassels, and beaded festoons are of carved wood gilded as are the brackets. These metal brackets are usually well formed with neat *bobèches* and sockets. This sconce has two scrolled branches. Above the horizontal pediment is placed an ornamental pedestal on which stands an alert and excellently modeled spread-eagle. The long vertical line of the grouped spears gives great distinction to this design. While the American Eagle seems to us paramount, and there were natural specimens at hand from which designers might model their birds, it is rare that they are handled on these fixtures as expertly as by English craftsmen. They are often quite primitive and crude.

Elaborately hung crystal sconces were a luxury but not uncommon. Some were of brass or bronze festooned in cut crystals but they do not compare favorably with English examples in the Adam style. Some were in the Empire style with a shaped backplate of French gilt, designed in patera form elaborately wreathed. From this small backplate the curved candle arms extended to the fanciful leaf-edged *bobèches* which were hung with the long glass prisms so popular in the mid-19th Century. These were evidently made to match the mantel candelabra, similarly designed with fringes of these long prisms.

Simple hanging lights for candles or lamps were still used in outlying districts, but in the cities and on the large estates very beautiful chandeliers were used as in England and France. Many of brass or bronze hung with glass and pendants in the Adam or French styles were still imported.

America's peculiar development was the lamp. Economic illumination became a study which has resulted in vast wealth from the use of kerosene, gas, and electricity. Camphene, a refined product of turpentine, highly explosive, was widely used about 1845–50. Previous to this sperm oil was general, and later kerosene. Lard and other greases and oils were used in outlying districts. Sperm oil was used until comparatively recent times in the household magic lantern. Many persons will recall its disagreeable odor. Common lamps were of tin, others of pewter, brass, bronze, occasionally iron, rarely pottery—one from the Bennington works being vase-shaped like those in other materials.

There is considerable variety in the shapes of the early brass lamps. Few are ornamented, but the most sprightly (Fig. 112) have well shaped oil fonts set on a short stem with a dished bottom, and a handle as engaging as one could wish in the form of an upturned dolphin. This is a further use of the dolphin ornament which was prevalent in glass candlesticks, clearly imitative— but oh, so clumsily, of those exquisite Venetian models which have captured the world to such an extent that a dolphin in glass seems to mean Venice.

While the early pewter lamps were very primitive, later examples made in the early 19th Century are often well shaped, but

112. A brass sperm oil lamp with a sprightly dolphin for a handle. 18th–19th Century. Courtesy The Metropolitan Museum.

rely mostly on the modeling of their stems for such comeliness as they possess. It is clear in most of them that designers did not yet know quite what to do with the lamp reservoir. This fact is plain in an early 19th Century pewter lamp (Fig. 113) with a cylindrical reservoir set on a short baluster with a well formed middle vase motif and sharp ringed turnings. The dished foot is in keeping with the baluster, but the handle is clearly an excrescence and the reservoir illy adjusted to its standard. The lamps that set directly on their bases are better conceived. The marine lamp (Fig. 114) is swung on pivots so it will right itself "when the ship goes wop, with a wiggle between." The glass lamps are very generally symmetrical in outline and often well designed. An old Sandwich molded glass lamp (Fig. 115) is for whale oil. Its hexagonal bowl is decorated with a star motif in a medallion; and its hexagonal baluster stem is in good proportion. The base too completes the lamp well. Another Sandwich glass lamp (Fig. 116) has its bowl ornamented with a pressed peacock decoration.

113. A curious mixture of elements in an early 19th Century pewter lamp. Courtesy The Metropolitan Museum.

114. A pewter marine lamp. Early 19th Century. Courtesy The Metropolitan Museum.

Its baluster stem is set on a well-shaped base. Both of these lamps are a little over ten inches in height. Some are of opaline glass.

Many glass lamps were imported, especially those of classic form like the Adam knife boxes used on sideboards. Such lamps were also silver-plated like those from Mount Vernon. It is possible that such lamps were imported in the late Colonial period. A pair of these lamps used by Washington (Fig. 117) has the oil font shaped and decorated in the Adam manner with a border and garlands. The lamp is placed well below the font, so that the oil will feed freely. The wall-plate is merely a disk, the entire beauty being centered in the oil font. Another interesting lamp from

115. Sandwich glass whale oil lamp, decorated in medallions. Courtesy The Anderson Galleries.

Mount Vernon (Fig. 118) is set on a glass base. The oil font is directly above this base and the lamps are set at both ends of a horizontal bar. This bar is nicely modeled, and the lamps braced with a simple scroll which extends from the stem below the bar. The total height of the lamp is 14½ in. Its type was preserved well into the 20th Century in the widely used Student's Lamp. A later type of Argand lamp (Fig. 119) became so well established that it was afterwards used as a gas drop-light. The larger of these lamps is of brass, with a tall fluted stem enriched with an embossed vine. It is topped by an acanthus corona and has a nice handling of the acanthus at its base. The pedestal is a tripod, reminiscent of the

Renaissance type, enriched by a cornice and decorated with lion-head masks. Its frosted glass shade is beautifully cut.

Thomas Jefferson is said to have imported the first Argand burner for his home "Monticello." Small wicks, broad flat wicks, and finally tubular wicks were used. New patents were constantly

116. Table lamp of Sandwich molded glass on hexagonal baluster stem, bowl with peacock decoration. Courtesy The Anderson Galleries.

117. One of a pair of silver-plated wall lamps used by Washingtan at Mount Vernon; urns of classic design. Courtesy United States National Museum.

coming out to improve the light: the "Solar Lamp," 1843, was a marked improvement. The "Astral Lamp" was invented by Count Rumford to overcome the shadow cast by the Argand burner. Great efforts were made to mount lamps decoratively on elaborate candelabra bases and in chandeliers; many were of bronze or glass hung with cut glass pendants. Much ingenuity was evident in

118. A silver-plated double lamp used by Washington at Mount Vernon; base of glass; total height 14½ in. Courtesy United States National Museum.

their design, with occasionally some beauty. They were handsomely made in pairs or sets of three. Tall table lamps were generally called astral lamps, but the name is properly applied to the type in which the oil font is held to the lamp burner by a horizontal arm. It often has a vase-shaped glass shade, and is not infrequently hung with glass pendants, as were the popular tall table lamps with brass or bronze standards which were set upon square bases of marble.

Lanterns of the finer sort were hung in the front hall at the foot of the stairs, plainer ones in back hallways. The more impressive lanterns were doubtless from England, but even these rarely achieved any great importance. Purely utilitarian lanterns were circular, semicircular, or rectangular; of tin, or other metal elaborately pierced or with glazed openings; and flat or coned tops with various shaped openings. Early lanterns, though distinctly utilitarian, are very often quite well-proportioned and effective though rarely decorative.

119. This type of tall Argand lamp was long popular, even after the advent of gas when it became the model for the drop-light. Courtesy American Art Association.

BACK OF THE PERIOD STYLES

BACK of all the beauty in the accomplishments of Italy, Spain, France, England, and America—the whole Western World, are those great sources, reservoirs, or fonts of development—China and Persia. Beauty is no vagrant but rather a continuous performance unfolding in the mind of man, although each nation has of course achieved its native and individual variant.

This continuity in design passing from nation to nation while

in the process of its evolution is palpably the idea upon which
Perrot and Chipiez based their series of art in the various nations,
beginning with Egypt and Mesopotamia and continuing down
through Judea, Persia and Greece. It is our recollection that they
rather neglected that gracious source of beauty and design—old
China, and unhappily they never reached Rome.

Properly and enjoyably to understand design as used in all
mediums, one should perhaps not necessarily begin with China
and Persia, but it is certain they should not be neglected. Eventu-
ally many streams lead back to their head-waters whence the
rivers of beauty uniting, refreshed and enriched Europe.

It seems rather foolish and uphill work to try to understand any
of the European *Period Styles* without a previous knowledge
of the older sources, for so many things are pleasantly familiar
when one does know them. The language of ornamental design
is perhaps the only universal language we possess. Of course it
is so inextricably interwoven with mythology, religion, history,
literature, and art as to make it rather forbidding to the novice,
but it is a knowledge that can be gathered crumb by crumb, and
every crumb counts even before you get the whole loaf.

Greek ornament is an open book written from one end of our
country to another especially on the outside and inside of our
older buildings. Egypt is housed in our larger museums and libra-
ries, with a corrupted word or two here and there in furnishings
made in the styles of the French Directorate and Empire. Persia
is astonishingly unknown except on our rugs, which is a crying
shame. It is not as readily available as it ought to be, though
many museums have isolated bits of this or that, which is entranc-
ing but not clearly illuminating until her art periods are understood. Something can be gleaned from books, something from art
catalogues, something and that often pleasantly from dealers—
we think appreciatively of Kelekian and Benguiat, of Dr. Khan,
the former Persian Minister at Washington; and something from
museum curators. But oh, how little of the whole ineffable beauty
of things Persian! We should know her pottery hanging lamps
better, especially her Rakka, more especially if blue glazed. Any

one who does not know Persia in her decorative modes does not know blue. Italy, Spain, France, England—how little they know of the ravishing beauty that is blue. We must go to Persia for that. Why! the heavenly blue on the Koubatcha plate on our own mahogany sideboard is worth all the blues of all Europe rolled into a precious bundle, and many of them are precious. We are not forgetting the blue on the lustered maiolica of Italy and Spain, made into candlesticks too at times.

Then China,—it is everybody's fault if he does not know China better. The Chinese are everywhere and they carry their legends in memory and know them well too. Even a laundryman or waiter in a restaurant knows more of the lore of the ages—Chinese ages, than a Caucasian college professor unless he is a specialist; for the laundryman and the waiter carry them in their hearts, a conscious heritage of their race. We have only recently reviewed a book on oriental art motifs crammed full of accumulated lore, easy to read a paragraph at a time, a page, or a full evening through.

Having unburdened ourselves of our plaint, we return to our theme. We repeat: that garnering in the fields of Asia, even Mesopotamia, India, Kotan—with Sir Aurel Stein if you will in his excavations of that precious territory where Persian, Chinese, and Greek art meet, you will appraise the European styles more accurately and enjoy them more fully wherever found, in lighting fixtures as in other furnishings.

How can you hope to value the metal arabesques on your candlestick if you do not know the damascening of the Near East! How is it possible to value the Capo di Monte figures on your chandelier, or the French porcelain figures on your girandole until you have seen and marveled at a rose-back plate or a pure white porcelain rice bowl from the Flowery Kingdom!

INDEX

INDEX